Cooking with Allie Always

Recipes from My Heart to Yours

Cooking With Allie Always
By Allie Always
Published by Allie Always, Barrington, NH

Copyright © 2025 Allie Always

All rights reserved.

This publication is protected under the U.S. Copyright Act of 1976 and all other applicable international, federal, state, and local laws, and all rights are reserved, including resale rights: you are not allowed to reproduce, transmit, or sell this book in part or in full without the written permission of the publisher.

For permission requests, write to the publisher, addressed "Attention: Allie Always, 181 Stagecoach Road, Barrington, NH 03825

Library of Congress Control Number: 2025915078

ISBN: 979-8-218-70532-9 (Hardcover)

Printed in the United States of America

10 9 8 7 6 5 4 3 2 1
First Edition

Dedication

To my amazing husband Corey, I couldn't have finished this without you. You're my rock and my best friend.

To my wonderful daughter, Izzy, thank you for always trying my dishes and even sometimes helping me in the kitchen. You're the light of my life.

Acknowledgments

This book would not exist without the incredible support, love, and encouragement I've received along the way.

To Corey and Isabella, thank you for being my biggest cheerleaders and the most enthusiastic taste testers I could ask for. Your encouragement made all the difference (and your honest feedback probably saved a few recipes, too!).

A heartfelt thank you to my parents, Priscilla Corliss and Bruce Faw. You both were incredible cooks; I cherish the memories of the food you put on our table. Thank you for raising me to be strong, resilient, and unafraid to follow my dreams. So much of who I am and what this book has become is because of you.

To both of my grandmothers, Ella Mae Faw and Lillian Corliss. Thank you for being such amazing cooks and for helping raise me with warmth, wisdom, and really good food. So much of this book is rooted in what you passed down to me.

To my editors, Colleen and Peter from Your Literary Prose, and my designer, Candy from WritingBytes. Your guidance, patience, and insight made this project better in every way. I truly couldn't have done this without you.

And to my wonderful friends, thank you for standing by me through every draft and every moment of doubt. Your support, encouragement, and cheers carried me through.

Allie and Corey in Tuscany, Italy

Forword

Cooking has been a part of our family's lives for as long as I can remember. I see my wife, Allison "Allie," in the kitchen, immersed in her craft. Her hands move with confidence, each chop and stir a reflection of years spent learning from her family, especially her Mamaw, "Ella Mae." It's more than just food; it connects to her roots in North Carolina and New Hampshire. Each recipe is a story, a memory, a piece of her heritage.

In Cooking with Allie Always, Allie shares her journey. This isn't just a collection of recipes; it's a guide to healthy living. She chooses the best of northern and southern cooking and transforms it into something accessible. The recipes are straightforward, allowing anyone to create nourishing and satisfying dishes.

What makes this book stand out is its focus on simplicity. Allie understands the challenges of everyday life. She knows how hard it can be to balance work, family, and health. Her approach is realistic. She offers meals that can be made quickly, using easily accessible ingredients.

Yet, it's not just about convenience. Allie's passion shines through each recipe. From hearty soups to vibrant salads, she emphasizes flavor without compromising health. You can taste her commitment to making cooking enjoyable and rewarding.

This book contributes to a broader conversation about nutrition and lifestyle. In a world where fast food often takes precedence, Allie invites us back to the kitchen. She encourages families to gather and share meals, nurturing connections that are so vital in today's fast-paced environment.

As you flip through the pages, you'll find more than just instructions. You'll discover a philosophy. Cooking can be an act of love, a moment of creativity, and a way to bring people together. I urge you to dive in, try the recipes, and make them your own. Let this book inspire you to create, savor, and share. Cooking with Allie isn't just about food; it's about building memories and fostering a healthier lifestyle for you and your loved ones.

Enjoy the journey ahead.

START OF THE DAY

Allie's Detox Green Juice	2
Banana, Oatmeal, Dark Chocolate Chip Bites	4
The Best Protein Bars	6
Allie's Avocado Toast	8
Chia Seed Pudding Bowls	10
Southern Sausage Gravy	12
Blueberry Muffins	14
Pecan Cinnamon Twists	16

DRESSINGS, SAUCES, RUBS, AND PICKLED

Apple Cider Vinaigrette Dressing	20
Balsamic Dressing	22
Avocado Dressing	24
Miso Dressing	26
North Carolina BBQ Sauce	28
Corey and Allie's BBQ Rub	30
Taco Seasoning	32
Beef Bone Broth	34
Fresh Basil Pesto	36
Pickled Jalapenos	38
Pickled Red Onions	40

STARTERS

Burrata Cheese Peaches on Sourdough	44
Tomato Confit Whipped Ricotta Cheese	46
Party Ranch Oyster Crackers	48
Spicy Maple Candied Bacon	50
Seven Layer Taco Dip	52
Guacamole	54
Cottage Cheese Party Dip	56
Whipped Ricotta and Heirloom Tomatoes	58
Tortellini Caprese Skewers	60
Pizza Pinwheels	62
Mango Salsa	64
Fresh Mex Tomatillo Salsa	66

Contents

Sides and Salads

Mexican Street Corn	70
Baked Macaroni and Smoked Cheese	72
Southern Green Beans and Salt Pork	74
Sauteed Snow Peas	76
Southern Coleslaw	78
Healthy Broccoli Slaw	80
Italian Pasta Salad	82
Greek Pasta Salad	84
Mediterranean Orzo Salad	86
Potato Salad	88
Baby Spinach and Berry Salad	90
Shrimp, Mango, and Avocado Salad	92
Fall Harvest Salad	94
Blueberry, Kale, Candied Pecan Salad	96
Mandarin Orange Salad	98
Watermelon and Tomato Salad	100
Taco Salad	102
Roasted Beet and Baby Kale Salad	104
Strawberry, Spinach, & Chicken Salad	106

Mains

Stuffed Peppers	152
Ham and Broccoli Quiche	154
Stuffed Butternut Squash	156
Butternut Squash Spinach Lasagna Rolls	158
Coconut Curry Shrimp Cilantro Lime Rice	160
Ground Turkey & Sweet Potato Skillet	162
Chicken Pot Pie	164
Cajun Shrimp Foils	166
Pan-Seared Scallops	168
Easy Mushroom Risotto	170
Chicken Tacos	172
Braised Beef Short Ribs	174
Beef Stew	176
Canadian Meat Pie (Tourtière)	178
Jambalaya	180
Chicken Cacciatore	182
Shrimp, Sausage, and Rice Skillet	184
Sweet Potato and Black Bean Burger	186

Bowls and Soups

Cali Shrimp Bowl	110
Crispy Chickpea Bowl	112
Harvest Bowl	114
Allie's Buddha Bowl	116
Roasted Sweet Potato Bowl with Farro	118
Potato and Leek Soup	120
Butternut Squash Soup	122
Cranberry and Apple Relish	124
Sausage Tortellini Soup	126
Coconut, Curry, Lime, & Chicken Soup	128
Beef, Cabbage, and Barley Soup	130
White Bean and Kale Soup	132
Roasted Tomato Soup	134
Chicken Noodle Soup	136
Split Pea and Ham Soup	138
Turkey, Mushroom, and Barley Soup	140
Pumpkin, Kale, and Quinoa Soup	142
Roasted Eggplant & Red Pepper Soup	144
Sweet Potato and Ground Turkey Chili	146
Chicken and White Bean Chili	148

Breads, Desserts, and Drinks

But You Ain't Ever Had My Cornbread	190
Focaccia Bread	192
Zucchini Chocolate Chip Bread	194
Chocolate Chip Banana Bread	196
Red Velvet Cupcakes	198
Pumpkin Bundt Cake Maple Pecan Glaze	200
Apple Crisp	202
Pistachio Cake with Icing	204
Pumpkin Pie	206
Mulled Apple Cider	208
Espresso Martini	210

Cooking with Allie Always

ALWAYS ALLIE

Introduction

My early childhood years were mainly spent in North Carolina, where we shared a home with my Mamaw and Papaw. I have favorite memories of being in the kitchen with my Mamaw, watching her make magic with simple ingredients. She made me a homemade country breakfast every morning, which included the most amazing buttermilk biscuits.

We also spent time in New Hampshire and made a final move there when I was 12 years old. We lived upstairs from my Grammy and Grampy, where my Grammy was also always in the kitchen. She made the best pancakes/crepes, and she made them for me all the time. While my grandmothers' cooking styles and food were different, both were masterful soup makers. I learned a great deal from them, yet it's interesting that I have never been able to replicate my grandmothers' biscuits or pancakes. I am committed to keep trying, but I am not sure they will ever taste as good as theirs.

I love how food brings people together and creates a sense of community; it's fun to share the love of food with one another. I love to give food to people, especially when they are under the weather; I will make soup and drop it off on their doorstep. I think of food as a way to be healthy and happy. When I'm in the kitchen, I'm incredibly happy. I always say that my secret ingredient is LOVE.

When I started typing my recipes into the computer, I thought this book would be for me and my daughter. I would hand it down to her because the recipes I had from family members were falling apart and hard to read. Once my husband saw the work I put into this book, he said, "You need to publish and share this with more people." It took a long time to agree to publish, because I was afraid of failing. Then I thought about how I always tell my daughter, "You must do hard things in life to succeed, and that is scary." So, here we are, and I'm happy to share my recipe book with you all.

> "Cooking does not have to be a chore, find fun in it. Put some music on, put a smile on your face and dance around while cooking. I promise you will begin to love it.

RECIPES IN THIS SECTION

- Allie's Detox Green Juice
- Healthy Banana, Oatmeal, and Dark Chocolate Chip Bites
- The Best Protein Bars
- Allie's Avocado Toast
- Chia Seed Pudding Bowls
- Southern Sausage Gravy
- Blueberry Muffins
- Pecan Cinnamon Twists

Start of the Day

Allie's Detox Green Juice

 This gorgeous green juice has become my go-to morning ritual. The sweetness of the green apples mellows out healthy kale and celery, while cucumber keeps it light and refreshing. I love how the cilantro adds unexpected brightness and the lemon pulls it together beautifully.

INGREDIENTS

- 4 STALKS CELERY
- 1 ENGLISH CUCUMBER
- 2 GREEN APPLES
- 1 LEMON
- 1 BUNCH CILANTRO
- 7 OUNCES FRESH KALE

PREPARATION

1. Clean all vegetables. Cut celery, cucumber, and apples into quarters.
2. Cut all the skin and pith off the lemon. (Pith is the white part under the skin)
3. Put all ingredients into an electric juicer.

   Enjoy!

Healthy Bites: Banana, Oatmeal, and Dark Chocolate Chip

» *These bites taste like a treat but are packed with the good stuff. The mashed bananas make them incredibly soft and naturally sweet, while those dark chocolate chips give you just enough indulgence to feel like you're having dessert. The oats and walnuts add a lovely texture.*

Ingredients

- 3 RIPE BANANAS, MASHED
- 2 CUPS QUICK OATS
- 1 CUP DARK CHOCOLATE CHIPS
- ¼ CUP CHOPPED WALNUTS
- 2 TBSP COCONUT MILK
- 1 TBSP CHIA SEEDS
- 1 TBSP HEMP HEARTS
- 1 TBSP MAPLE SYRUP
- 1 TSP VANILLA EXTRACT
- 1 TSP CINNAMON

Preparation

1. Preheat oven to 375°F.
2. Mash the bananas in a large bowl. Then add all the remaining ingredients and mix well to combine.
3. Line a cookie sheet with parchment paper. Use a cookie scoop to form balls. Then place the cookies on a sheet about 4 inches apart.
4. Bake for 15 minutes or until firm.

   Enjoy!

The Best Protein Bars

PREPARATION

1. Combine vanilla, honey, peanut butter, and coconut oil in a saucepan over low heat. Stir every few minutes until ingredients are well combined, around 10 minutes.

2. While the mix is heating, place almonds, walnuts, pecans, cashews, and dates in a food processor and chop until the mixture resembles coarse sand. Do not overmix, or it will result in nut butter.

3. Add shredded coconut and sunflower seeds and pulse a few times until the sunflower seeds are rough chopped. Place mixture in a mixing bowl.

4. Remove the melted mixture from the stove, then stir in the nut mixture.

5. Line 12 x 8-inch baking dish with parchment paper, pour the bar mixture into the dish.

6. Put another piece parchment on top and use palms to press mixture evenly into the pan. Pack it down tightly. This will help the bars bind and not crumble. Remove top parchment paper add chocolate chips on top; press them lightly into the mixture.

7. Set in freezer for 2 hours. Lift the bottom parchment paper with the bars out of the pan and put on cutting board. Use a sharp knife to cut into rectangle-shaped bars.

8. Store in refrigerator for 2 weeks or individually wrap and place the bars in a freezer bag for a few months. Remove bars from freezer about 20 minutes prior to serving. Enjoy!

INGREDIENTS

2 TSP VANILLA

1/2 CUP RAW HONEY

1 CUP NATURAL UNSWEETENED PEANUT BUTTER

1/4 CUP COCONUT OIL

1 CUP RAW ALMONDS

1 CUP RAW WALNUTS

1 CUP RAW PECANS

1 CUP RAW CASHEWS

10 MEDJOOL DATES, PITTED

1/2 CUP UNSWEETENED SHREDDED COCONUT

1/2 CUP SNFLOWER SEEDS

1/2 CUP DARK CHOCOLATE CHIPS

RECIPE BOOK

Allie's Avocado Toast

 The creamy avocado with a hint of lime and garlic makes a perfect base, but it's really the fresh mozzarella and sweet tomatoes that take it over the top—it's like having a caprese salad on toast! I love the peppery bite from the arugula and how that balsamic glaze ties everything together with the right touch of sweetness.

INGREDIENTS

2 SLICES OF BREAD (I LIKE TO USE SOURDOUGH BREAD)

1 RIPE AVOCADO

1 WEDGE OF LIME

1 PINCH GARLIC POWDER

BUNCH OF BABY ARUGULA

½ CUP CHOPPED TOMATOES

½ CUP FRESH MOZZARELLA, CUT INTO BITE-SIZED PIECES

3 BASIL LEAVES, CHOPPED

1 TBSP BALSAMIC GLAZE STORE-BOUGHT IS GREAT

SALT AND PEPPER TO TASTE

PREPARATION

1. Toast bread to a nice brown and crunch.
2. Mash the avocado and mix it with lime, garlic powder, and salt and pepper to taste.
3. Spread the mixture on toast.
4. Layer baby arugula, tomatoes, mozzarella, and basil, and drizzle with balsamic glaze.

Enjoy!

Chia Seed Pudding Bowl

 I love how tiny chia seeds transform overnight into a creamy, tapioca-like texture. The vanilla and touch of honey make it taste like dessert, but I I'm getting fiber and omega-3s. Some mornings I'll top it with fresh berries and a sprinkle of coconut, other days it's chopped pecans and whatever fruit we have on hand.

PREPARATION

1. Pour Chia seeds, almond milk, honey, and vanilla into a covered container.
2. Shake to mix well. Store in the fridge overnight.
3. Shake often.
4. When ready to enjoy, add any fruits, nuts, and coconut flakes.
5. List your favorite combination of toppings below!

   Enjoy!

INGREDIENTS

2 TBSP CHIA SEEDS

½ CUP ALMOND MILK OR COCONUT MILK (BOTH UNSWEETENED)

1 TSP HONEY OR REAL MAPLE SYRUP

1 TSP REAL VANILLA EXTRACT

BERRIES, OTHER FRUIT, UNSWEETENED COCONUT FLAKES, AND NUTS

Southern Sausage Gravy

INGREDIENTS

1 16-OUNCE PACKAGE JIMMY DEAN REGULAR PORK SAUSAGE

2 TBSP BUTTER

2 TBSP ALL-PURPOSE FLOUR

2 CUPS WHITE MILK

1/4 TSP BLACK PEPPER

1/8 TSP SALT

PREPARATION

1. Add the pork sausage to a cast-iron skillet and cook over medium heat, breaking it up into small pieces, until cooked through.

2. Remove cooked pork from skillet with a slotted spoon and place it on a paper towel-lined plate.

3. Wipe remaining oil from skillet with a paper towel, add the butter and flour, and cook the roux for about 2 minutes, whisking continuously.

4. Slowly whisk the milk into the roux, making sure to pull up all the bits from the skillet. Add the salt and pepper.

5. Continue to cook and stir until mixture simmers and thickens, add the sausage back into the mixture.

6. You may need to add a extra milk and continue cooking until reaching your desired consistency for gravy.

7. Check seasoning; adjust if needed.

8. Sausage gravy is best served right away on biscuits and eggs.

   Enjoy!

As a young girl growing up in North Carolina, sausage gravy was a staple in my home. My father made it with ground hamburger meat, a method he learned in the Air Force, where it was called S.O.S. My Mamaw would use pork sausage, and it honestly did not matter what she used, because her cooking was magical. Now, when I make it, I use seasoned pork such as Jimmy Dean.

Blueberry Muffins

PREPARATION

1. Preheat oven to 400°F. Line a muffin tin with paper liners.

2. In a medium-sized bowl, whisk together flour, sugar, baking powder, baking soda, and salt.

3. In a separate bowl, whisk together milk, butter, eggs, and vanilla.

4. Add wet ingredients to dry and gently fold together until batter is mostly combined. Add the frozen blueberries and continue to combine. Do not overmix.

5. Divide the muffin batter evenly into lined muffin tins. Sprinkle with Turbinado sugar.

6. Bake for 25 to 30 minutes, or until a toothpick inserted into the center of the muffins comes out clean.

7. Allow the muffins to cool for a few minutes and enjoy while warm.

    Enjoy!

INGREDIENTS

2 CUPS ALL-PURPOSE FLOUR

1 CUP SUGAR

2 TSP BAKING POWDER

½ TSP BAKING SODA

¼ TSP SALT

½ CUP MILK

½ CUP UNSALTED BUTTER, MELTED

2 LARGE EGGS, ROOM TEMPERATURE

2 TSP VANILLA EXTRACT

2 CUPS FROZEN BLUEBERRIES, NOT THAWED

TURBINADO SUGAR FOR SPRINKLING ON TOP

Pecan Cinnamon Twists

 Pecan cinnamon twists are hands down one of my favorite guilty pleasures. I owe the recipe to my friend and coworker, Sarah Todd. I have a soft spot for anything made with puff pastry, so when I tried these for the first time, I was instantly hooked. The combination of cinnamon, pecans, and a light, flaky puff pastry makes them absolutely irresistible. It's one of my go-to recipes, and I love making them for friends and family; they are always a hit.

INGREDIENTS

¼ CUP LIGHT BROWN SUGAR

¼ CUP PECAN HALVES

½ TSP CINNAMON

1 9 x 10-INCH SHEET PUFF PASTRY, THAWED

1 LARGE EGG, BEATEN

PREPARATION

1. Combine sugar, pecans, and cinnamon in a food processor until a sandy texture is achieved.

2. Line a baking sheet with parchment paper. Preheat oven to 400°F.

3. Unfold puff pastry, brush with beaten egg.

4. Spread sugar mixture over the puff pastry; using a pizza cutter, cut the puff pastry into ½-inch-wide strips.

5. Fold each strip in half and twist. Place on parchment-lined baking sheet, push the ends down with your thumb.

6. Freeze for 10 minutes or until firm.

7. Bake for 18 to 20 minutes or until golden brown. Cool on the rack and enjoy warm.

Enjoy!

RECIPES IN THIS SECTION

- Apple Cider Vinaigrette Dressing
- Balsamic Dressing
- Avocado Dressing
- Miso Dressing
- North Carolina BBQ Sauce
- Corey and Allie's BBQ Rub
- Taco Seasoning
- Beef Bone Broth
- Fresh Basil Pesto
- Pickled Jalapenos
- Pickled Red Onions

Dressings, Sauces, Rubs, and Pickled

> **Condiments are like old friends, highly thought of, but often taken for granted.**
> ...Marilyn Kaytor

Apple Cider Vinaigrette Dressing

PREPARATION

1. Add all ingredients to a Mason jar or a salad dressing shaker.

2. Place the lid on the jar tightly, and shake until all ingredients are well combined.

3. It's best to make it ahead of time to allow the flavors to blend well.

4. Shake well before using.

   Enjoy!

INGREDIENTS

½ CUP OLIVE OIL

¼ CUP APPLE CIDER VINEGAR

1 TBSP DIJON MUSTARD

1 TBSP AGAVE NECTAR

1 TSP MINCED GARLIC

½ TSP SALT

¼ TSP PEPPER

Balsamic Dressing

INGREDIENTS

½ CUP OLIVE OIL

¼ CUP BALSAMIC VINEGAR

2 TBSP HONEY

1 TBSP GARLIC, MINCED

1 TBSP DIJON MUSTARD

SALT AND PEPPER

PREPARATION

1. Add all ingredients to a Mason jar or a salad dressing shaker.

2. Place the lid on the jar tightly, and shake until all ingredients are well combined.

3. It's best to make it ahead of time to allow the flavors to blend well.

4. Shake before each use.

    Enjoy!

Avocado Dressing

PREPARATION

1. In a blender, combine the avocado, cilantro, lime juice, olive oil, water, salt, and cumin.

2. Blend until smooth.

3. If the consistency is thick, adjust by adding more water.

   Enjoy!

INGREDIENTS

1 RIPE AVOCADO

1 CUP CILANTRO LEAVES

1 LIME, JUICED

¼ CUP EXTRA VIRGIN OLIVE OIL

¼ CUP WATER

¼ TSP SALT

¼ TSP CUMIN

Miso Dressing

INGREDIENTS

- **1** TBSP WHITE MISO
- **2** TBSP RICE VINEGAR
- **2** TBSP SESAME OIL
- **1** TSP AGAVE NECTAR
- **1** TSP SOY SAUCE
- **1** TSP FRESH GRATED GINGER
- **1** TSP FRESH-PRESSED GARLIC
- **1** TSP SRIRACHA
- **1/3** CUP OF OLIVE OIL
- **1/3** CUP OF WATER

PREPARATION

1. Add all ingredients into a Mason jar or a salad dressing shaker.
2. Place the lid on the jar tightly, and shake until all ingredients are well combined.
3. It's best to make it ahead of time to allow the flavors to blend well together.
4. Shake before each use.

   Enjoy!

North Carolina BBQ Sauce

PREPARATION

1. Add all the ingredients to a small saucepan.
2. Bring to a boil, then reduce to a simmer, cooking for 2 minutes until sugar and salt dissolve.
3. Remove from heat and let cool.
4. Strain through a sieve and store in a squeeze bottle in the refrigerator until ready to use.
5. It can be stored for up to three weeks. Enjoy!

INGREDIENTS

1 CUP APPLE CIDER VINEGAR

1 CUP OF WATER

2 TBSP KETCHUP

2 TBSP BROWN SUGAR

1 TSP RED PEPPER FLAKES

1 TSP BLACK PEPPER

1/2 TSP SALT

I'm not sure if it's because I grew up in North Carolina, but I've never liked a sticky-sweet BBQ sauce. To me, this is the way BBQ should be, especially for pulled pork.

Everyone in the North slathers the thick BBQ sauce on everything, and I think that takes away from the true flavor. Whenever I introduce this vinegar-based BBQ sauce to my friends in the North, they are all blown away by it and immediately ask for the recipe.

RECIPE BOOK

Corey and Allie's BBQ Rub

INGREDIENTS

- 1/3 cup brown sugar
- 2 tsbp paprika
- 1 tsbp smoked paprika
- 1 tsbp onion powder
- 1 tsbp garlic powder
- 1 tsbp black pepper
- 1 tsbp salt
- 1 tsp mustard powder
- ¼ tsp cayenne pepper

PREPARATION

1. Mix all ingredients together. Store in an airtight container and keep in a spice rack until ready to use.

2. When putting a rub on any kind of meat, apply the rub 24 hours in advance and refrigerate.

   Enjoy!

Taco Seasoning

 Tacos are one of my favorite foods to eat, and I love making them. When I was younger and first started making tacos, I bought the premade seasoning packs from the store. Every time I ate them, they made me feel ill. It made me sad, so I researched why and what to do. I found the natural ingredients in taco seasoning and put them together to create the best taco seasoning mix with no additives. I cannot imagine making them any other way.

PREPARATION

1. In a small bowl, add all ingredients and mix until combined.
2. Store in an airtight container for up to six months.

   Enjoy!

INGREDIENTS

1 TBSP CHILI POWDER

2 TSP GROUND CUMIN

1 TSP PAPRIKA

1 TSP SALT

1 TSP GROUND BLACK PEPPER

½ TSP GARLIC POWDER

½ TSP DRIED OREGANO

Beef Bone Broth

 Bone broth is like liquid gold in my kitchen. I love how simple it is. Those beef bones release their goodness slowly, creating a deep, nourishing broth for sipping or using as the base for soups and stews. It's funny how something our grandmothers did out of necessity is now a trendy superfood, but honestly, they knew what they were doing! I always keep some in the freezer because it makes everything from risotto to gravy taste richer.

INGREDIENTS

4 TO 5 POUNDS OF BEEF BONES (THIS IS GREAT WHEN YOU HAVE LEFTOVER BONES FROM PRIME RIB)

1 ONION, QUARTERED

2 CARROTS, CUT INTO LARGE PIECES

2 CELERY STALKS, CUT INTO LARGE PIECES

2 CLOVES GARLIC

2 BAY LEAVES

10 PEPPERCORNS

1 TBSP SALT

HANDFUL OF PARSLEY, CHOPPED

PREPARATION

1. Put all ingredients in a stock pot and bring to a boil.

2. Cover the pot, reduce heat to low, and cook for 12 to 24 hours.

3. Strain the bone broth, discarding the solids.

4. Taste, and, if desired, add more salt and pepper.

5. Use right away (up to 3 days) or store in a freezer-safe container and freeze up to three months.

Enjoy!

Fresh Basil Pesto Sauce

PREPARATION

1. Wash basil, pick only the leaves off the stems, and place in a food processor.

2. Add Parmesan cheese, pine nuts, garlic, and salt and pepper to taste to the food processor.

3. Place the lid on the food processor; turn on to start mixing. Remove the smaller insert to add the olive oil.

4. Start adding olive oil slowly. Blend for 1 minute. Take the top of the food processor off and scrape down the sides. Place the lid back on, turn on, and add more olive oil if needed.

5. Once completely blended to the desired consistency, taste and add salt or pepper, if needed.

6. This pesto can be added to pasta, pizza, soup, bread, or butter on top of chicken. Pesto can also be frozen and saved for later use.

   Enjoy!

INGREDIENTS

3 CUPS FRESH BASIL (NO STEMS)

½ CUP PARMESAN CHEESE

¼ CUP PINE NUTS

2 TBSP GARLIC, CRUSHED

SALT AND PEPPER TO TASTE

¼ CUP OLIVE OIL, PLUS MORE FOR A SMOOTHER PESTO

Pickled Jalapenos

INGREDIENTS

12 JALAPEÑOS, SLICED

1 CUP BRAGG APPLE CIDER VINEGAR

1 CUP WATER

1/3 CUP CANE SUGAR

1 TBSP GARLIC, CRUSHED

1 TBSP SEA SALT

PREPARATION

1. Slice jalapenos and place in a large canning jar.
2. In a saucepan, combine apple cider vinegar, water, cane sugar, garlic, and salt.
3. Simmer for 10 minutes.
4. Immediately pour pickling liquid over jalapenos, cover with a tight lid and place in the refrigerator.
5. Enjoy in approximately 10 days.
6. The jalapenos last approximately two months refrigerated.

    Enjoy!

Pickled Red Onions

PREPARATION

1. In a saucepan, combine apple cider vinegar, water, sugar, salt, garlic, and peppercorns.

2. Simmer ingredients for 10 minutes and let sit.

3. While your ingredients are simmering, slice red onion into thin slices and place in a large Mason jar.

4. You might need two jars.

5. Place a sieve or cheesecloth, over the onions and pour hot liquid into the jar(s).

6. Place the lid on the Mason jar and place in the refrigerator; enjoy in 24 hours.

7. These will last up to two weeks in the fridge.

   Enjoy!

INGREDIENTS

1 LARGE RED ONION

1 CUP BRAGG APPLE CIDER VINEGAR

1 CUP WATER

¼ CUP SUGAR

1 TBSP SALT

1 TBSP GARLIC, CRUSHED

1 HANDFUL WHOLE PEPPERCORNS

RECIPE BOOK

RECIPES IN THIS SECTION

- Burrata Cheese and Peaches on Sourdough Bread
- Tomato Confit with Whipped Ricotta Cheese
- Party Ranch Oyster Crackers
- Spicy Maple Candied Bacon
- Seven Layer Taco Dip
- Guacamole
- Cottage Cheese Party Dip
- Whipped Ricotta and Heirloom Tomatoes
- Tortellini Caprese Skewers
- Pizza Pinwheels
- Mango Salsa
- Fresh Mex Tomatillo Salsa

Starters

> **Cooking is art. May you create masterpieces in your kitchen.**

Burrata Cheese and Peaches on Sourdough Bread

PREPARATION

1. Butter each side of the sliced sourdough bread, and place in preheated cast-iron pan or flattop.

2. Grill until each side becomes crispy and light brown.

3. Peel and slice the peaches.

4. Once the sourdough is browned, top each slice with 1/2 of a burrata ball and spread it along the bread.

5. Top with sliced peaches, drizzle with balsamic glaze, and add a pinch of thyme, salt, and pepper.

   Enjoy!

INGREDIENTS

SOURDOUGH BREAD, SLICED

RIPE PEACHES, SLICED

BURRATA CHEESE

BALSAMIC GLAZE, STORE-BOUGHT

DRIED THYME

SALT AND PEPPER

Tomato Confit with Whipped Ricotta Cheese

INGREDIENTS

1 PINT CHERRY TOMATOES

1 TBSP OLIVE OIL

1 TBSP GARLIC, CRUSHED

1 TSP FRESH THYME

2 CUPS WHOLE MILK RICOTTA CHEESE

¼ CUP PARMESAN CHEESE, GRATED

1 TBSP HONEY

1 TBSP FRESH LEMON JUICE

1 TSP FRESH BASIL, CHOPPED

1 TSP SALT

¼ TSP PEPPER

FOCACCIA BREAD
(SEE PAGE 192 FOR THE RECIPE)

PREPARATION

1. In a skillet over medium heat, add the cherry tomatoes, olive oil, garlic, fresh thyme, salt, and pepper.

2. Cook over medium heat until tomatoes start to break apart and become soft.

3. In a food processor, combine ricotta cheese, Parmesan cheese, honey, lemon juice, thyme, and salt and pepper to taste.

4. Combine and blend the ingredients until the mixture is very smooth.

5. First, place the ricotta cheese mixture on a serving dish, then layer the tomato confit and sprinkle with freshly chopped basil.

6. Serve with warm focaccia bread.

   Enjoy!

ALWAYS ALLIE

Party Ranch Oyster Crackers

 This recipe is from my mother-in-law, Cindy. She makes these crackers around the holidays and gives everyone a bag. My husband and daughter love them so much that I asked Cindy for the recipe, so I could make them more often and continue the tradition of these delicious crackers. She was happy to share, now I am happy to share this fond memory and recipe.

PREPARATION

1. Preheat the oven to 250°F.
2. In a small bowl, whisk together oil, ranch dressing mix, dill weed, and garlic powder.
3. Place oyster crackers in a large bowl and pour the oil mixture over the oyster crackers.
4. Use a spatula to incorporate and coat all the oyster crackers onto a large baking sheet and place in the oven.
5. Bake for 10 to 15 minutes, then stir and bake another 10 to 15 minutes.
6. Remove from the oven, allow to cool.
7. Store in a sealed container.

   Enjoy!

INGREDIENTS

1 CUP OIL

1 PACKAGE OR 2 TSBP HIDDEN VALLEY RANCH DRESSING MIX

1 TSP DILL WEED

¾ TSP GARLIC POWDER

2–16-OUNCE BAGS OF SMALL OYSTER CRACKERS

RECIPE BOOK

Spicy Maple Candied Bacon

 This recipe comes from my dear friend Karen Townsend. When our families get together, we enjoy wonderful food and fabulous drinks. We hosted Easter 2018 at our home. The Townsends brought ultimate Bloody Mary beverages. One of the accoutrements was an amazing candied bacon. Spicy and sweet always hits the spot. In my opinion, these were the best Bloody Mary drinks we have ever had.

INGREDIENTS

1 LB. THICK CUT APPLEWOOD SMOKED BACON, LOCAL IF POSSIBLE

2-½ TBSP PACKED BROWN SUGAR

2 TBSP MAPLE SYRUP

1-½ TSP CHIPOTLE CHILI POWDER

PREPARATION

1. Preheat the oven to 350°F, set a rack in the middle position.
2. Line a baking sheet with aluminum foil or parchment paper.
3. Set an oven-safe rack on top of the baking sheet.
4. Place bacon in a single layer on the rack. Bake for 20 minutes.
5. While the bacon is in oven, in a small bowl, stir together the brown sugar, syrup, and chipotle powder; set aside.
6. Remove pan from oven and flip bacon slices over. Spread the sugar mixture evenly over all slices of bacon. Place pan back into oven for 20-30 minutes.
7. It might take more or less time depending on the cut of the bacon; check the bacon often. Let cool and serve. Enjoy!

Seven Layer Taco Dip

PREPARATION

1. Spread refried beans in an even layer on the bottom of your serving dish.
2. In a separate medium bowl, combine the sour cream, lime juice, and taco seasoning.
3. Spread over refried beans in an even layer.
4. You can make this combination ahead of time if you have the time to spare.
5. Make your guacamole and spread it in an even layer over the sour cream mixture.
6. Spread the salsa in an even layer over the guacamole.
7. Sprinkle cheese evenly over salsa.
8. Top with shredded lettuce, tomatoes, and black olives.
9. Serve with tortilla chips.

   Enjoy!

INGREDIENTS

16-OUNCE CAN REFRIED BEANS

16-OUNCE SOUR CREAM

½ LIME, JUICED

2-½ TBSP TACO SEASONING (SEE PAGE 32 FOR RECIPE)

2 CUPS GUACAMOLE (TURN THE PAGE FOR RECIPE)

1-½ CUPS TACO CHEESE, SHREDDED

16 OZ. CHUNKY SALSA

2 CUPS LETTUCE, SHREDDED

½ CUP TOMATOES, CHOPPED

½ CUP SLICED BLACK OLIVES

TORTILLA CHIPS FOR SERVING

Guacamole

INGREDIENTS

3 AVOCADOS

1 LIME, JUICED

2 TBSP FRESH CILANTRO, FINELY CHOPPED

½ TSP GARLIC POWDER

½ TSP SALT

½ TSP GROUND BLACK PEPPER

PREPARATION

1. Cut avocados in half, take the pit out, and peel.
2. Mash the insides of avocados with a fork or potato masher, leaving some chunks.
3. Add lime juice, cilantro, garlic powder, salt, and pepper, and mix until combined.
4. If you make it in advance, squeeze a little lime juice over the top, place plastic wrap directly on the top of the guacamole, and refrigerate. Enjoy!

Cottage Cheese Party Dip

PREPARATION

1. Add all ingredients into a medium-sized bowl and mix well.

2. Cover and place in the fridge for several hours.

3. Serve with townhouse crackers or any crackers of your choice.

   Enjoy!

INGREDIENTS

24 OUNCES COTTAGE CHEESE

½ CUP COCKTAIL SAUCE

1 TBSP WORCESTERSHIRE SAUCE

1 TBSP CHOPPED PARSLEY

1 TSP GARLIC POWDER

GROUND PEPPER TO TASTE

Whipped Ricotta and Heirloom Tomatoes

INGREDIENTS

2 CUPS WHOLE MILK RICOTTA CHEESE

¼ CUP PARMESAN CHEESE, GRATED

1 TBSP HONEY

1 TBSP FRESH LEMON JUICE

1 TBSP FRESH THYME

2 LARGE HEIRLOOM TOMATOES

1 TBSP OLIVE OIL

1 TBSP FRESH BASIL, CHOPPED

SALT AND PEPPER TO TASTE

BALSAMIC GLAZE, STORE-BOUGHT

PREPARATION

1. In a food processor, combine ricotta cheese, Parmesan cheese, honey, lemon juice, thyme, and salt and pepper to taste.

2. Combine ingredients until the mixture is very smooth.

3. Cut heirloom tomatoes into bite-sized pieces.

4. Place on a serving plate and drizzle with olive oil, balsamic glaze, salt and pepper to taste.

5. Place the whipped ricotta next to the tomatoes on the serving dish; sprinkle with fresh, chopped basil.

6. Another great item to serve with is toasted sourdough bread.

    Enjoy!

Tortellini Caprese Skewers

PREPARATION

1. Cook the tortellini according to the package instructions.

2. Once cooked, place in a bowl with a little olive oil and let cool.

3. Once the tortellini are cooled, begin assembling the skewers.

4. I like to use large, knotted bamboo skewers.

5. Assemble in this order: tortellini, basil leaf, grape tomato, mozzarella ball.

6. Place on a platter; drizzle with balsamic glaze.

7. Serve cold and enjoy!

INGREDIENTS

10-OUNCE BAG OF FRESH CHEESE TORTELLINI OR OTHER FRESH TORTELLINI

1 FRESH BUNCH OF BASIL

1 PINT GRAPE TOMATOES

8 OUNCES FRESH MOZZARELLA CILIEGINE BALLS

1 FRESH BUNCH OF BASIL

BALSAMIC GLAZE, STORE-BOUGHT

OLIVE OIL

RECIPE BOOK

Pizza Pinwheels

Ingredients

1 can refrigerated pizza dough

½ cup pizza sauce

1 cup mozzarella cheese

Any other pizza topping you might want

(If your topping is pepperoni or peppers, I recommend precooking; it's always a good idea to precook).

Preparation

1. Preheat oven to 400°F. Line the bottom of a baking sheet with parchment paper.
2. Roll out dough on a wooden cutting board. I use a drinking glass to roll out dough; it keeps it from sticking.
3. Spread pizza sauce evenly over the dough to the edges.
4. Top with mozzarella and any choice of toppings.
5. Roll the pizza dough into a log shape, sealing the ends, then slice it into 1-inch pieces.
6. Place pinwheels on the cookie sheet about 2 inches apart.
7. Bake at 400°F for about 15-20 minutes or until the top of the pinwheel is golden brown. The time can vary depending on your oven.
8. Plate, allow to cool, and serve with a side of pizza sauce.

    Enjoy!

Mango Salsa

PREPARATION

1. In a bowl, combine all prepared ingredients and mix well.

2. If you have time, it's best to make this an hour before serving.

3. The extra time allows the flavors of all ingredients time to incorporate.

Tip: This salsa is amazing and pairs perfectly with fish such as salmon or fish tacos.

INGREDIENTS

3 RIPE MANGOS, DICED

1 RED BELL PEPPER, CHOPPED

¼ CUP FRESH CILANTRO, CHOPPED

1 JALAPENO, SEEDED AND CHOPPED

1 LIME, JUICED

1 TSP GARLIC, MINCED

¼ TSP SALT

RECIPE BOOK

Fresh Mex Tomatillo Salsa

>> This salsa first showed up at a Cinco de Mayo party when a friend brought it along, and it instantly stole the show. Bright, zesty, and full of flavor, everyone went crazy for it. I knew it was too good to forget, so I had to learn how to make it myself and give it a permanent place in my recipe book.

INGREDIENTS

1-½ POUNDS TOMATILLOS (AROUND 12), HUSKED AND RINSED

2 MEDIUM JALAPENOS, STEMMED

1 SWEET ONION, CUT IN HALF

2 CLOVES OF GARLIC

½ CUP CILANTRO LEAVES, FRESH

2 MEDIUM LIMES, JUICED

1 TSP SALT

DRIZZLE OF OLIVE OIL

PREPARATION

1. Preheat oven to 400°F.
2. Line a baking sheet with parchment paper.
3. Add the whole tomatillos, stemmed jalapenos, halved onion, and whole garlic cloves.
4. Drizzle with olive oil and a little salt.
5. Roast for 20 minutes, turning halfway through.
6. Remove from oven.
7. Peel garlic. Deseed jalapenos. Rough chop the onion.
8. In a food processor, add all roasted ingredients, cilantro, lime juice, and salt.
9. Pulse until all ingredients are chopped to the desired consistency. Enjoy!

RECIPES IN THIS SECTION

- Mexican Street Corn
- Baked Macaroni and Smoked Cheese
- Southern Green Beans with Salt Pork
- Sautéed Snow Peas and Bell Peppers
- Southern Coleslaw
- Healthy Broccoli Slaw
- Italian Pasta Salad
- Greek Pasta Salad
- Mediterranean Orzo Salad
- Potato Salad
- Baby Spinach and Berry Salad
- Shrimp, Mango and Avocado Salad
- Fall Harvest Salad
- Blueberry, Kale, and Candied Pecan Salad
- Mandarin Orange Salad
- Watermelon and Tomato Salad
- Taco Salad
- Roasted Beets and Baby Kale Salad
- Strawberry, Spinach and Chicken Salad

Sides and Salads

> **Always do what you love, and Always have fun doing it.**

RECIPE BOOK

Mexican Street Corn

 This recipe comes from our good friends Julie and Kevin. We were having a home cookout, and asked everyone to bring a side dish. Julie and Kevin brought this street corn and blew us away with this dish. I told them right away I needed this recipe so I could have it more often, and I am sure every guest there night asked for the recipe.

PREPARATION

1. Heat grill or smoker to 400°F; be sure the grates are clean.
2. In a medium-sized bowl, whisk together crema, mayonnaise, cilantro, garlic, chipotle pepper, and lime juice.
3. Season to taste, if needed; (this dish can be made ahead of time and kept in the refrigerator).
4. Rub down the corn with olive oil. Grill the corn for about 5 minutes, or until the kernels start to brown; turn it over and repeat on all sides.
5. Once done, place on a plate.
6. Using a brush or spoon, coat each ear of corn with the crema mixture. Sprinkle with crumbled cotija cheese.
7. Serve immediately with a lime wedge and Enjoy!

INGREDIENTS

8 MEDIUM EARS SWEET CORN, HUSKS REMOVED

½ CUP MEXICAN CREMA OR SOUR CREAM

½ CUP MAYONNAISE

½ CUP CILANTRO, MINCED

1 CLOVE GARLIC, MINCED

¼ TSP CHIPOTLE CHILI POWDER

2 TBSP LIME JUICE

½ CUP COTIJA CHEESE, CRUMBLED

LIME WEDGES TO SERVE

OLIVE OIL

Baked Macaroni and Smoked Cheese

INGREDIENTS

2 SLICES SOURDOUGH BREAD, TORN INTO PIECES

1 TBSP OLIVE OIL

4 CUPS ELBOW MACARONI

2 TBSP BUTTER

2 TBSP FLOUR

2 CUPS MILK

¼ TSP DRY MUSTARD

DASH OF CAYENNE PEPPER

¼ TSP SALT

2 CUPS GRATED SHARP CHEDDAR CHEESE

1 CUP GRATED SMOKED GOUDA CHEESE

PREPARATION

1. Preheat oven to 400°F.
2. Tear bread into pieces, add to food processor, and process to make breadcrumbs.
3. Drizzle olive oil over crumbs and stir until all crumbs are moistened.
4. Bring water to a boil and cook macaroni for about 7 minutes (or according to package instructions).
5. Melt butter in a saucepan over medium heat. Sprinkle in the flour and whisk until well blended with the butter.
6. Cook this roux for a few minutes. Whisk in milk, dry mustard, cayenne, and salt.
7. Bring to boil, whisking continuously, lower heat and simmer for 30 seconds.
8. Remove from heat and stir in cheeses.
9. Drain macaroni. Spoon macaroni into a shallow casserole dish. Pour cheese sauce over macaroni and toss well. Sprinkle on the breadcrumbs.
10. Bake for 15 minutes or just until sauce is sizzling, and crumbs begin to brown.

    Enjoy!

ALWAYS ALLIE

I first discovered this baked macaroni with smoked cheese in the most unexpected place, a work cafeteria! I was around thirty, already a big fan of macaroni and cheese, when I saw a coworker warming up the most amazing-looking leftovers I'd ever laid my eyes on. I asked her for the recipe right then and there. That was twenty years ago, and I've been making it ever since. The smoky, cheesy richness hooked me from the start, and it's one of my most requested dishes whenever there's a get-together. It's pure comfort food with a little something extra that makes it unforgettable. The recipe's secret is the smoked Gouda.

Southern Green Beans with Salt Pork

PREPARATION

1. Place butter and salt pork in cast-iron Dutch oven and sauté for five minutes.

2. Add green beans, chicken stock, apple cider vinegar, garlic, bouillon, sugar, and pepper.

3. Cover and braise on low heat for three hours, being sure to check every half hour or so.

4. If the liquid dries up, add a little water, but not too much.

Enjoy!

INGREDIENTS

1 TBSP BUTTER

1 3-INCH SLICE OF SALT PORK

2 LBS. FRESH GREEN BEANS, CUT INTO 1-½ INCH PIECES

4 CUPS CHICKEN STOCK

2 TBSP APPLE CIDER VINEGAR

1 TBSP GARLIC, MINCED

1 TBSP BETTER THAN BOUILLON, CHICKEN FLAVOR

1 TBSP SUGAR

1 TSP GROUND PEPPER

Southern green beans with salt pork always bring back memories from my childhood, when Mamaw would simmer them low and slow until the house was filled with an unmistakable, savory aroma. That smell alone meant a good meal was coming, comforting and full of love. I hadn't tasted anything quite like it in years, until a recent trip to North Carolina brought those flavors rushing back. I was inspired to recreate them myself, and after experimenting, came up with my version. Now, they're a hit, and it feels like bringing a piece of my childhood to the table again.

RECIPE BOOK

Sautéed Snow Peas and Bell Peppers

INGREDIENTS

1 TBSP SESAME OIL

1 TBSP OLIVE OIL

15-OUNCE BAG SUGAR SNAP PEAS

1 YELLOW BELL PEPPER, SLICED THINLY

1 RED BELL PEPPER, SLICED THINLY

1 TBSP GARLIC, MINCED

SALT AND PEPPER TO TASTE

TOASTED SESAME SEEDS (OPTIONAL)

PREPARATION

1. Heat a large skillet over medium heat. Add olive oil and sesame oil to the pan; swirl to coat the pan.

2. Add sugar snap peas, all sliced bell peppers, garlic; add salt and pepper.

3. Sautee for 10 to 15 minutes, or until peppers are tender.

4. Remove from heat, place in dish, and serve warm.

Enjoy!

Tips: If the pan starts to dry out while cooking, just add a little water.

If you're able to eat toasted sesame seeds, add them before being served.

This combination of crisp sugar snap peas and sweet bell peppers creates a rainbow on the plate. It's funny how something so simple can make the whole meal feel more special, and it pairs beautifully with everything from grilled chicken to pot roast.

Southern Coleslaw

> There's nothing quite like a good Southern coleslaw. The secret to mine is simple; let it sit for a little while before serving so all the flavors can marry together, the cabbage softens just right, the dressing soaks in, and it becomes the perfect, classic Southern side dish that belongs at every cookout or family table no matter where you live.

PREPARATION

1. In a large bowl, mix together the onion, mayonnaise, sugar, vinegar, mustard, and celery seed; add salt and pepper to taste.

2. Add mixture to coleslaw mix and toss until well-coated.

3. Refrigerate for an hour before serving.

    Enjoy!

INGREDIENTS

1 TBSP GRATED SWEET ONION

1 CUP DUKE'S MAYONNAISE

2 TBSP SUGAR

2 TBSP APPLE CIDER VINEGAR

2 TBSP BROWN MUSTARD

2 TSP CELERY SEEDS

1 16-OUNCE BAG COLESLAW MIX

SALT AND PEPPER TO TASTE

Healthy Broccoli Slaw

Ingredients

¼ cup olive oil

1 tbsp honey

1 tbsp rice wine vinegar

1 tbsp brown mustard

¼ tsp celery seeds

1 12-ounce bag shredded broccoli and carrots

½ cup raisins

½ cup sunflower seeds

salt and pepper to taste

Preparation

1. In a small bowl or jar, mix olive oil, honey, rice wine vinegar, brown mustard, and celery seeds.

2. Add salt and pepper to taste. Set aside.

3. Combine shredded broccoli and carrots, raisins, and sunflower seeds in a large bowl.

4. Add dressing and toss.

5. Refrigerate for an hour before serving.

Enjoy!

Italian Pasta Salad

 This Italian pasta salad is a lifesaver for summer gatherings. It feeds a crowd and gets better as it sits! Sometimes I'll add cucumber or switch up the cheese depending on what's in the fridge. This one never fails to disappear completely!

INGREDIENTS

- 1 LB. UNCOOKED ROTINI PASTA
- 1 PACKAGE GRAPE TOMATOES, CUT IN HALF
- 8 OUNCES FRESH MOZZARELLA CHEESE PEARLS
- 8 OUNCES SALAMI, CUT INTO CUBES
- 1 BELL PEPPER, DICED
- 1 CUP SLICED BLACK OLIVES
- ½ CUP PARMESAN CHEESE, GRATED
- ¾ CUP PEPPERONCINI, CHOPPED
- ½ CUP FRESH PARSLEY, CHOPPED
- 1 CUP OLIVE GARDEN'S SIGNATURE ITALIAN DRESSING OR BALSAMIC DRESSING (RECIPE ON PAGE 22)
- SALT AND PEPPER TO TASTE

PREPARATION

1. Cook pasta according to the directions on the box.
2. Drain cooked pasta and transfer to a bowl. Cool in the refrigerator for 10 minutes.
3. While pasta is cooking and cooling, prepare all items to add to the salad.
4. Once pasta is cooled, add all prepared ingredients and mix well.
5. This salad can be served right away, or it can be made a day or two in advance.

Enjoy!

RECIPE BOOK

Greek Pasta Salad

 Greek or Italian. Honestly, I can never decide which one I love more! Where the Italian salad has a rich, hearty feel with salami and mozzarella, this Greek version is fresh and bright with tangy feta cheese and briny kalamata olives to wake up your whole palate. It's funny how switching from Basalmic dressing to Greek and swapping a few ingredients can take you on a completely different flavor journey.

INGREDIENTS

- 16 ounces small bow tie pasta
- 1 English cucumber, diced
- 1 pint grape tomatoes, halved
- 1 bell pepper (yellow or orange), diced
- 1 jar kalamata olives, sliced
- 1 cup feta cheese, crumbled
- 1 cup bottled Greek dressing

PREPARATION

1. Cook pasta, following directions on the package; drain and cool.
2. Once pasta is cool, add all ingredients and toss.
3. Refrigerate for 1-2 hours before serving.
4. It's good to incorporate all the ingredients into the dressing.

Enjoy!

Mediterranean Orzo Salad

Ingredients

- 2 cups uncooked orzo pasta
- 1 pint grape tomatoes, sliced in half
- 1 English cucumber, diced
- 1 red bell pepper, diced
- 1 3.5-ounce jar capers, drained
- 1 6-ounce jar sliced Kalamata olives, drained
- 1 cup parsley, chopped

Ingredients for Dressing

- 1 lemon, juiced
- ¼ cup olive oil
- 2 tbsp white wine vinegar
- 1 tsp garlic, minced
- 1 tsp dried oregano
- Feta cheese, to your liking

Preparation

Instructions for Dressing

1. Put all dressing ingredients into a Mason jar and shake well to incorporate all ingredients.

Instructions for Salad

1. Cook orzo pasta, following directions on the package.
2. Drain and rinse with cold water.
3. Add all salad ingredients and dressing to a large bowl.
4. Mix well and refrigerate for 2 hours or overnight.

Enjoy!

Southern Potato Salad

INGREDIENTS

4 LBS. BABY YUKON GOLD POTATOES

4 HARD-BOILED EGGS, PEELED AND CHOPPED

3 CELERY STALKS, CHOPPED

½ CUP SWEET ONION, SHREDDED

1-½ CUPS DUKE'S MAYONNAISE

1 CUP SWEET PICKLE RELISH

1 TBSP YELLOW MUSTARD

1 TBSP DIJON MUSTARD

1 TBSP APPLE CIDER VINEGAR (BRAGG'S BRAND IS THE BEST)

1 TSP CELERY SEEDS

½ TSP PAPRIKA

SALT AND PEPPER TO TASTE

PREPARATION

1. Place potatoes in a large pot. Add cold water to 1 inch over potatoes. Add salt and bring to boil for 15-20 minutes, or until fork tender. At the same time prepare the eggs.

2. While the potatoes are cooking, mix the mayonnaise, relish, mustards, apple cider vinegar, celery seeds, salt and pepper to taste in a large bowl.

3. Add the celery, onions, and the prepared eggs and whisk until smooth. and incorporate them well. Keep in the refrigerator until the potatoes are ready.

4. When potatoes are tender, strain and chill them in the fridge for a few hours.

5. Once potatoes are cool enough to handle, remove peels or leave them on (your choice), cut into ½-inch chunks, place in a large mixing bowl.

6. Add dressing; gently fold until well incorporated. Sprinkle paprika on top.

7. Cover and refrigerate. This salad is best if you can make it a day in advance.

Enjoy!

Tip: If you're making this in advance, wait to add the paprika when served.

ALWAYS ALLIE

>> My Southern Potato Salad has earned a spot as one of my most beloved recipes. It's creamy, tangy, and full of that down home comfort only a true Southern dish can bring. The two key ingredients that take it from good to unforgettable are Bragg's apple cider vinegar for that perfect zing, and Duke's mayonnaise for its savory flavor. It's sure to be a hit every time you serve it.

Baby Spinach and Berry Salad

INGREDIENTS

1 PINT BLUEBERRIES

1 PINT BLACKBERRIES

1 PINT RASPBERRIES

1 LB. FRESH STRAWBERRIES, CHOPPED

1 TBSP BAKING SODA

1 16-OUNCE PACKAGE BABY SPINACH

1 23.5-OUNCE JAR MANDARIN ORANGES, DRAINED

½ CUP PECANS, CHOPPED, OPTIONAL

½ CUP FETA OR GOAT CHEESE, OPTIONAL

BALSAMIC DRESSING

PREPARATION

1. Soak all berries in a bowl of water and baking soda. Rinse, drain, and spin in a salad spinner (spin slower than normal).

2. Rinse the baby spinach; use a salad spinner to dry it.

3. In a large salad bowl, layer baby spinach, all berries, and mandarin oranges; top with pecans or almond slices and cheese of your choice.

4. Add balsamic dressing (on page 22).

   Enjoy.

Shrimp, Mango, and Avocado Salad

INGREDIENTS

1 LB. LARGE SHRIMP, PEELED AND DEVEINED

1 FRESH PACKAGE BABY SPINACH

1 ENGLISH CUCUMBER, DICED

2 AVOCADOS, DICED

2 MEDIUM MANGOES, DICED

1 PACKAGE MATCHSTICK CARROTS

SALT AND PEPPER

PREPARATION

1. Place cleaned shrimp on skewers and sprinkle with salt and pepper.

2. Grill until the shrimp turns pink and opaque.

3. Start to arrange salad – baby spinach, diced cucumbers, diced avocados, diced mango, matchstick carrots, and shrimp.

4. Top with your favorite dressing.

   Enjoy!

Fall Harvest Salad

PREPARATION

1. Preheat oven to 400°F.

2. Place cubed butternut squash in a large bowl with olive oil, thyme, salt, and pepper. Toss until the butternut squash is coated with the mixture.

3. Place butternut squash on a parchment-lined baking sheet. Roast in oven 15 minutes, flip pieces then take out and move around on baking sheet. Place back in oven to roast for 15 more minutes. Set aside to cool.

4. In a large bowl, toss kale, cooled roasted butternut squash, cubed apple, dried cranberries, pecans, and feta until combined.

5. Top with apple cider vinaigrette (found on page 20).

Enjoy!

INGREDIENTS

1 SMALL BUTTERNUT SQUASH, CUT INTO ½-INCH CUBES

1 TBSP OLIVE OIL

1 TSP THYME

½ TSP SALT

¼ TSP GROUND PEPPER

1 HONEYCRISP APPLE, CUBED

1 PACKAGE FRESH BABY KALE

½ CUP DRIED CRANBERRIES

1 CUP PECANS, ROASTED AND CHOPPED

½ CUP FETA CHEESE

Autumn wrapped in one gorgeous bowl! The roasted butternut squash becomes sweet and caramelized in the oven, and paired with those crisp Honeycrisp apples and tangy dried cranberries, it's the best flavors of the season in every bite. The roasted pecans add the perfect crunch. The feta brings salty balance to the natural sweetness, and pairs perfectly with the homemade apple cider vinaigrette.

Blueberry, Kale, and Candied Pecan Salad

INGREDIENTS PECANS PREPARATION

6 TBSP PACKED BROWN SUGAR

1 TSP GROUND CINNAMON

½ TSP SALT

½ TSP VANILLA EXTRACT

PINCH CAYENNE PEPPER

1 TBSP WATER

2 CUPS PECAN HALVES

1. Line a baking sheet with parchment paper.

2. Add brown sugar, cinnamon, salt, vanilla, cayenne, and water to a saucepan over medium heat. Stir often until sugar melts and bubbles for 1 minute.

3. Stir in the pecans and coat them with the brown sugar mixture, cook over low heat until the pecans smell nutty; around 3-4 minutes. Watch and stir the nut and sugar mixture often so the nuts do not burn.

4. Use a slotted spoon to transfer the nuts to the baking sheet and arrange in one layer. Let the pecans cool. Serve immediately or keep in an airtight container at room temperature for up to one week.

INGREDIENTS SALAD PREPARATION

1-½ BUNCHES CURLY LEAF KALE

1-½ CUP FRESH BLUEBERRIES

½ CUP CRUMBLED FETA

1 CUP CANDIED OR PLAIN PECANS

1. Wash and strip all the leaves from the stems of the kale; roughly chop.

2. Place chopped kale in a large bowl and toss with your hands to soften it a bit. Then add balsamic dressing (found on page 22) to the kale and toss until mixed.

3. Top with blueberries, feta, and pecans.

   Enjoy!

ALWAYS ALLIE

Mandarin Orange Salad

INGREDIENTS

1 23.5-OUNCE JAR MANDARIN ORANGES, DRAINED

8 OUNCES BABY GREEN LEAF LETTUCE

¾ CUP DRIED CRANBERRIES

¾ CUP ALMONDS, SLICED

1 4-OUNCE BAG TORTILLA STRIPS

PREPARATION

1. In a large bowl, toss lettuce, mandarin oranges, dried cranberries, and almonds until combined.

2. Add a protein of your choice, toss with your favorite dressing, and top with tortilla strips.

Enjoy!

Watermelon and Tomato Salad

 On a trip to Montréal, we had this unforgettable watermelon and tomato salad. It was juicy, sweet, tangy, topped with crumbled feta and a rich balsamic reduction. I couldn't stop thinking about it; the flavors stayed with me like a dream I wanted to remember. I decided to create my own version, and it turned out to be just as refreshing and delicious. Now it's one of my daughter's favorite salads, and every time I serve it, every taste brings back that perfect day in Canada.

INGREDIENTS

1 SEEDLESS WATERMELON, CUT INTO 1-INCH CHUNKS OR USE A MELON BALLER

2 CUPS GRAPE TOMATOES, CUT IN HALF

2 TBSP BALSAMIC VINEGAR

2 TBSP AGAVE NECTAR

1 BUNCH MINT, CHOPPED

1 CUP FETA

SALT AND PEPPER TO TASTE

BALSAMIC GLAZE, STORE-BOUGHT

PREPARATION

1. Gently mix watermelon, tomatoes, balsamic vinegar, agave nectar, and salt and pepper to taste in a nonreactive bowl.

2. Cover the mixture and place it in the refrigerator for 1 hour, stirring every fifteen minutes.

3. After an hour, place the mixture in a strainer and let all the juices drain.

4. Place the strained watermelon-tomato mixture in a serving bowl, add mint and feta, and toss gently.

5. Drizzle with a balsamic glaze.

   Enjoy!

RECIPE BOOK

Taco Salad

INGREDIENTS

1 ONION, CHOPPED INTO SMALL PIECES

1 LB. ORGANIC GROUND BEEF

½ TSP EACH OF CHILI POWDER, PAPRIKA, CUMIN, AND GARLIC POWDER

2 HEADS OF ROMAINE LETTUCE WASHED, DRIED, AND CHOPPED

1 CUP FROZEN CORN, THAWED

6-OUNCE CAN SLICED BLACK OLIVES, DRAINED

15-OUNCE CAN OF BLACK BEANS, DRAINED AND RINSED

1 PINT GRAPE TOMATOES, SLICED

1 AVOCADO, DICED

SALT AND PEPPER TO TASTE

PREPARATION

Beef Instructions

1. In a skillet over medium heat, add onions and cook for 2 minutes; add ground beef. Cook until the meat is brown.

2. Drain grease from beef. Add beef back to the skillet, then add the chili powder, paprika, cumin, garlic powder, and salt and pepper to taste; stir until combined.

Salad Instructions

1. To prepare salad, start with romaine lettuce, add ground seasoned beef, corn, black olives, black beans, tomatoes, and avocado.

2. Dress with Avocado Dressing (recipe found on page 24).

   Enjoy!

Roasted Beets and Baby Kale Salad

INGREDIENTS

6 MEDIUM BEETS (SCRUBBED AND WASHED WITH VEGGIE BRUSH)

2 TBSP OLIVE OIL

1 TBSP BALSAMIC VINEGAR

1 CUP WHOLE PECANS

1 PACK OF PREPACKAGED BABY KALE

1 APPLE, CORED AND CHOPPED

1 CUP FETA CHEESE

SALT AND PEPPER TO TASTE

PREPARATION

1. Preheat oven to 400°F.

2. Place the washed beets in a baking dish and drizzle with olive oil, balsamic vinegar, and season with salt and pepper to taste.

   Roast for 1 hour, then let it cool.

3. In a pan, toast the pecans over medium heat with no oil, stirring constantly until they are brown. Set aside.

4. Once beets are cool, peel them and cut into bite-sized pieces.

5. In a serving bowl, place kale, roasted beets, apple, pecans, and feta cheese and mix.

6. Top with balsamic dressing (page 22)

   Enjoy!

Tip: When cutting up the beets, it's a good idea to wear kitchen-safe gloves.

Strawberry, Spinach, and Chicken Salad

PREPARATION

1. In a pan, toast almonds with no oil over medium heat, stirring constantly until brown.

2. Set aside.

3. Grill chicken strips, cool, and chop into bite-sized pieces.

4. Assemble salad: place spinach in a large salad bowl.

5. Add strawberries, avocado, chicken, almonds, and cheese.

6. Add your favorite dressing.

   Enjoy!

INGREDIENTS

¾ CUP SLICED ALMONDS, TOASTED

2 LBS. CHICKEN STRIPS

5 OUNCES BABY SPINACH, WASHED AND READY TO USE

1 QUART STRAWBERRIES, HULLED AND QUARTERED

1 AVOCADO, PEELED AND CHOPPED

¾ CUP GORGONZOLA CHEESE

To me, this is pure summer on a plate! The combination of juicy strawberries with tender grilled chicken is divine, and I love how the creamy avocado and tangy gorgonzola balance each other. I started making this when I was trying to get my family excited about eating more salads, and now my daughter actually asks for it!

RECIPE BOOK

RECIPES IN THIS SECTION

- Cali Shrimp Bowls
- Crispy Chickpea Bowl
- Harvest Bowl
- Allie's Buddha Bowl
- Roasted Sweet Potato Bowl with Farro
- Potato and Leek Soup
- Butternut Squash Soup
- Cranberry and Apple Relish
- Sausage Tortellini Soup
- Coconut, Curry, Lime, and Chicken Soup
- Beef, Cabbage, and Barley Soup
- White Bean and Kale Soup
- Roasted Tomato Soup
- Chicken Noodle Soup
- Split Pea and Ham Soup
- Turkey, Mushroom, and Barley Soup
- Pumpkin, Kale, and Quinoa Soup
- Roasted Eggplant and Red Pepper Soup
- Baby Spinach and Berry Salad
- Sweet Potato and Ground Turkey Chili
- Chicken and White Bean Chili

Bowls, Soups, and Chilis

> "Life is too short to eat boring food.

Cali Shrimp Bowls

PREPARATION

1. Cook rice and let it cool a bit, then add rice vinegar.

2. Combine the mayonnaise and sriracha; you can thin it a bit with water if it's too thick.

3. Divide prepared rice between 4 bowls. Top with cucumbers, shrimp, and avocado.

4. Drizzle soy sauce and mayonnaise-sriracha mixture.

5. Top with sesame seeds.

   Serve and enjoy!

INGREDIENTS

1 CUP SHORT-GRAIN BROWN RICE

3 TBSP RICE VINEGAR

¼ CUP MAYONNAISE

1 TSP SRIRACHA SAUCE

1 ENGLISH CUCUMBER, DICE

8 OUNCES COOKED SHRIMP, REMOVE TAILS AND CHOP INTO SMALL PIECES

2 AVOCADOS, MASHED

1 TSP FRESH CHIVES, CHOPPED

4 TSP SESAME SEEDS

4 TSP REDUCED-SODIUM SOY SAUCE

RECIPE BOOK

Crispy Chickpea Bowl

INGREDIENTS

1 15-OUNCE CAN CHICKPEAS

2 TBSP PURE SESAME OIL

1 TBSP WHITE OR YELLOW MISO PASTE

2 TSP MAPLE SYRUP

1/2 TSP RED PEPPER FLAKES

BOWL INGREDIENTS

2 CUPS BROWN RICE OR QUINOA

SHREDDED RED CABBAGE

DICED CUCUMBER

DICED RED BELL PEPPERS

DICED CARROTS

1/4 CUP ROASTED PEANUTS, FINELY CHOPPED

WEDGE OF LIME

MISO DRESSING, PAGE **26**

PREPARATION

1. Prepare grains, following instructions on the package.

2. Preheat oven to 425°F (218 C).

3. Rinse and drain chickpeas, then pat very dry with a towel—this will help them crisp up.

4. In a medium mixing bowl, add oil, miso paste, maple syrup, and red pepper flakes, and whisk until combined, then add chickpeas and toss to coat.

5. Arrange on a parchment-lined baking sheet; bake for 20-25 minutes, tossing/stirring once at the halfway point to ensure even baking. They're done when crisp and a deep golden brown. Set aside.

6. Prepare Miso Dressing.

7. Prepare all vegetables and toppings at this time and set aside.

8. To serve, divide grains between serving bowls and top with chickpeas, red cabbage, diced cucumber, red bell peppers, carrots, peanuts, lime wedge, and dressing.

Enjoy!

Harvest Bowl

PREPARATION

1. Cook farro following the directions on the package. Preheat the oven to 400°F.

2. Wash and cut the delicata squash in half, clean out the middle, and discard. Lay each half face down and cut into even slices. Place the squash in a bowl.

3. Open chickpeas and add to colander, rinse well, and dry with a towel. Add the chickpeas to the same bowl as the delicata squash. Drizzle olive oil; add thyme. Salt and pepper to taste.

4. Place parchment paper on baking a sheet. Pour squash, chickpeas onto baking sheet.

5. Rinse broccolini and place on separate parchment paper-covered baking sheet. Drizzle with olive oil; salt and pepper.

6. Place both baking sheets in the oven and bake for 20 minutes. After 10 minutes, remove the baking sheets from the oven, and stir and turn ingredients. Return baking sheets to the oven and finish baking.

7. To serve, place cooked farro at the bottom of a bowl, then place squash, broccolini, chickpeas, and pepitas on top of farro.

8. Top with a premade tahini sauce or peanut sauce dressing.

9. If you want to add a protein, this pairs well with grilled chicken or fish.

   Enjoy!

INGREDIENTS

1 CUP FARRO

1 DELICATA SQUASH

1 CAN CHICKPEAS, RINSED

1 TBPS OLIVE OIL

¼ TSP THYME

1 BUNCH BROCCOLINI

½ CUP PEPITAS

SALT AND PEPPER TO TASTE

RECIPE BOOK

Allie's Buddha Bowl

INGREDIENTS

(You can put almost any yummy ingredient in these bowls.)

8 hard-boiled eggs

1 cup brown rice or quinoa

1 lb. grilled chicken

1 bunch of kale, chopped or torn into chip-size pieces

1 bunch asparagus

2 tbsp olive oil

Salt and pepper to taste

PREPARATION

1. Preheat oven to 350°F.
2. Boil eggs to your desired hardness, peel, and cut in half.
3. Cook brown rice or quinoa, following directions on the package.
4. Salt and pepper chicken then grill.
5. Drizzle chopped kale with olive oil and sprinkle with salt and pepper to taste.
6. Cut asparagus into bite-sized pieces, drizzle with olive oil, and sprinkle with salt and pepper.
7. Spread seasoned kale on a cookie sheet, place in oven, and check every few minutes until the kale has turned crispy.
8. Place asparagus on a cookie sheet and roast in the oven for 15 minutes.
9. In a bowl, layer rice or quinoa, grilled chicken, asparagus, hard-boiled eggs, and top with kale chips and your favorite dressing.

Enjoy!

Roasted Sweet Potato Bowl with Farro

PREPARATION

1. Preheat the oven to 400°F.

2. Toss the sweet potato cubes with olive oil, salt, and pepper. Roast until golden brown for about 30 minutes.

3. Cook farro, following directions on the package.

4. Plate or bowl farro and sweet potatoes.

5. Add the greens, carrots, apple, and almonds.

6. Finish with Apple Cider Vinaigrette (recipe on page 20).

INGREDIENTS

2 SWEET POTATOES, CHOPPED INTO CUBES

1 CUP FARRO

2-3 CUPS SALAD GREENS

2 CARROTS, PEELED INTO RIBBONS

2 APPLES, DICED

½ CUP SLICED ALMONDS

Potato and Leek Soup

INGREDIENTS

3 TBSP UNSALTED BUTTER

4 LARGE LEEKS, WHITE AND LIGHT GREEN PARTS ONLY, ROUGHLY CHOPPED (ABOUT FIVE CUPS), SOAKED, RINSED, AND STRAINED

3 CLOVES GARLIC, PEELED AND SMASHED

2 POUNDS YUKON GOLD POTATOES, PEELED AND ROUGHLY CHOPPED INTO 1/2-INCH PIECES

7 CUPS LOW SODIUM CHICKEN BROTH

2 BAY LEAVES

3 SPRIGS FRESH THYME

1 TEASPOON SALT

1/4 TSP GROUND BLACK PEPPER

1 CUP HEAVY CREAM

CHIVES, FINELY CHOPPED, FOR SERVING

PREPARATION

1. Melt butter on medium heat in large pot.
2. Add the leeks and garlic, and cook, stirring regularly, until soft and wilted, about 10 minutes.
3. Adjust the heat as needed to prevent burning.
4. Add the potatoes, broth, bay leaves, thyme, salt, and pepper to the pot and bring to a boil.
5. Cover pot, turn heat down to low.
6. Simmer for 20 minutes or until the potatoes are soft.
7. Remove thyme sprigs and bay leaves, then purée the soup with a handheld immersion blender until smooth.
8. Add heavy cream, bring to a simmer.
9. Taste and adjust seasoning with salt and pepper.
10. If the soup is too thin, simmer it until it thickens.
11. If it's too thick, add water or stock to thin it. Garnish with fresh chives, if desired.

Enjoy!

Butternut Squash Soup with Cranberry and Apple Relish

PREPARATION

1. To a large pot, add butternut squash, onion, apple, vegetable broth, garlic, ginger, sage, rosemary, salt, and pepper.

2. Cook on medium heat until all ingredients become soft.

3. Add a full sprig of rosemary and let it cook for another 15 minutes.

4. Turn the heat off and let the mixture sit in the pot for 30 minutes.

5. Remove the rosemary sprig.

6. Add maple syrup and heavy cream to the soup mixture and blend with an immersion blender until smooth.

7. Serve with a cranberry and apple relish. (Recipe on the next page)

   Enjoy!

INGREDIENTS

2 LBS. BUTTERNUT SQUASH, PEELED, SEEDED, AND CUBED

1 SWEET ONION, CHOPPED

1 GRANNY SMITH APPLE, PEELED, CORED, AND CHOPPED

4 CUPS VEGETABLE BROTH

1 TBSP GARLIC, MINCED

1 TBSP GINGER, GRATED GINGER

5 LEAVES OF FRESH SAGE

1 SPRIG OF FRESH ROSEMARY

½ TSP SALT AND PEPPER

1 TBSP MAPLE SYRUP

½ CUP HEAVY CREAM

RECIPE BOOK

Cranberry and Apple Relish

INGREDIENTS

1 MEDIUM GRANNY SMITH APPLE, PEELED, CORED, AND DICED

1 CUP OF DRIED CRANBERRIES, CHOPPED

1 TBSP APPLE CIDER

1 TSP OLIVE OIL

1 TSP CHILI POWDER

1 TSP MAPLE SYRUP

SALT AND PEPPER TO TASTE

PREPARATION

1. Assemble all the ingredients.
2. Mix them well.
3. Then, let them sit in the fridge for 30 minutes to one hour before serving with butternut squash.

Enjoy!

» This hearty, flavor-packed Sausage Tortellini Soup has earned its place as one of my most requested dishes. Every fall, our friends Ray and Kristen host a cozy, laughter-filled soup party, and this is the one I always bring to the party. Rich, savory broth, tender cheese-filled tortellini, and perfectly seasoned sausage come together to make a bowl of pure comfort. It's the kind of soup that gets people asking for the recipe time and time again.

Sausage Tortellini Soup

PREPARATION

1. Make 1-inch meatballs from the Italian sausage.

2. Add olive oil and sausage balls to a Dutch oven and cook over medium heat until browned.

3. Remove meatballs, place on a paper towel-lined plate, and discard rendered fat.

4. Add carrots, celery, and onion. Cook for five minutes.

5. Add garlic, thyme, oregano, basil, salt, and pepper. Cook for another minute.

6. Add broth, tomatoes, tomato sauce, and kale; bring to a simmer over medium heat until carrots are tender (about 15 minutes).

7. Add tortellini, cover and simmer for 5 minutes. Serve and enjoy.

Tip: You can use pearl couscous instead of cheese tortellini.

INGREDIENTS

1 LB. SWEET ITALIAN SAUSAGE, GROUND

1 TBSP OLIVE OIL

3 CARROTS, PEELED AND SLICED

3 STALKS OF CELERY, CHOPPED

1 LARGE ONION, CHOPPED

1 TBSP GARLIC, MINCED

½ TSP EACH THYME, OREGANO, AND BASIL

1 TSP OF SALT AND PEPPER

4 CUPS CHICKEN STOCK OR VEGETABLE STOCK

1 14-OUNCE CAN DICED TOMATO

¼ CUP OF TOMATO SAUCE

1 CUP CHOPPED KALE (CAN USE FROZEN)

20 OUNCES OF FRESH CHEESE TORTELLINI

Coconut, Curry, Lime, and Chicken Soup

INGREDIENTS

1.5 LBS. BONELESS CHICKEN BREAST

1 TBSP OLIVE OIL

1 ONION

2 RED BELL PEPPERS, CHOPPED

3 SMALL CARROTS, PEELED AND SLICED

13-OUNCE CAN LIGHT COCONUT MILK

1 LIME, JUICED

32 OUNCES CHICKEN STOCK

1 TBSP CURRY POWDER

1 CUP WHITE RICE

¼ CUP CHOPPED CILANTRO

SALT AND PEPPER TO TASTE

PREPARATION

1. In a medium-sized saucepan, boil the chicken in water for 15 mins, take the pan off the burner, and let sit in the water until it has cooled slightly.

2. In a large pot, add olive oil, onion, bell peppers, and carrots, and sauté for 5 minutes.

3. Add coconut milk, lime juice, chicken stock, curry powder, and salt and pepper to taste.

4. Take the chicken out of the water and cut into small pieces; add it to the soup.

5. Add rice and simmer on low heat for 20 minutes or until rice is done. Add chopped cilantro and serve.

Enjoy!

Beef, Cabbage, and Barley Soup

INGREDIENTS

- 1 TBSP OLIVE OIL
- 2 LBS. CHUCK ROAST, CUT INTO CUBES
- 8 CUPS BEEF BROTH
- 1 MEDIUM ONION, CHOPPED
- 1 TBSP GARLIC, MINCED
- 1 14.5-OUNCE CAN DICED TOMATOES
- 2 TBSP WORCESTERSHIRE SAUCE
- 2 TBSP TOMATO PASTE
- 2 BAY LEAVES
- 3 MEDIUM CARROTS, PEELED AND SLICED
- 2 STALKS CELERY, CHOPPED
- 2/3 CUP BARLEY
- 3 CUPS CABBAGE, SHREDDED

PREPARATION

1. Add olive oil to the Dutch oven and heat over medium heat.
2. Place the cubed chuck roast in the Dutch oven and start to brown (sear).
3. Once browned, add 4 cups of beef broth, onions, garlic, diced tomatoes, Worcestershire sauce, tomato paste, and bay leaves.
4. Let this cook on low heat for 2 hours; this mixture can simmer for a very long time (this is how you get the beef to fall apart).
5. Once the beef is cooked and falling apart, add the remaining beef broth, carrots, celery, and barley. Let this cook for 30 minutes.
6. Add cabbage and cook for another 30 minutes.

Enjoy.

White Bean and Kale Soup

INGREDIENTS

- 1 TBSP OLIVE OIL
- 1 LARGE ONION, CHOPPED
- 2 CARROTS, PEELED AND CHOPPED
- 1 GARLIC CLOVE, MINCED
- 4 CUPS VEGETABLE BROTH
- 3 14-OUNCE CANS WHITE BEANS, DRAINED AND RINSED
- 1 14-OZ CAN DICED TOMATOES
- 4 CUPS CHOPPED KALE
- 1 TSP THYME
- SALT AND PEPPER TO TASTE

PREPARATION

1. In a large pot, heat olive oil over medium heat.
2. Add onions, carrots, and garlic; cook for 5 minutes.
3. Mash one can of beans in a small dish.
4. Add mashed beans and broth to the pot and bring to a boil.
5. Stir in remaining beans, diced tomatoes, kale, thyme, and salt and pepper to taste.
6. Reduce heat and simmer until kale is tender.

Enjoy!

Roasted Tomato Soup

PREPARATION

1. Preheat oven to 400°F.

2. Line two baking sheets with parchment paper. Place tomato halves, garlic, and onion on baking sheets. Drizzle with olive oil and season with salt and pepper.

3. Roast in the oven for 40 to 50 minutes or until tomatoes start to split.

4. Once tomatoes, garlic, and onions are done roasting, let them rest for 10 or 15 minutes.

5. When they have cooled down, transfer them to a food processor and blend for two minutes. Add the basil and blend for another two minutes.

6. Once the ingredients are completely blended, transfer the mixture to a large pot over medium heat.

7. Add oregano, sugar, and vegetable broth. Add salt and pepper to taste.

8. Simmer on low heat for 30 minutes. Serve with croutons or grilled cheese.

    Enjoy!

INGREDIENTS

3 LBS. ROMA TOMATOES, CUT IN HALF

1 HEAD GARLIC, TOP CUT OFF

1 SWEET ONION, THICK SLICED

4 TBS OLIVE OIL

1/2 CUP BASIL LEAVES

1/2 TSP OREGANO

1 TBPS SUGAR

2 CUPS VEGETABLE BROTH

SALT AND PEPPER TO TASTE

Chicken Noodle Soup

INGREDIENTS

2 TBSP OLIVE OIL

1 MEDIUM ONION, CHOPPED

2 CELERY STALKS, DICED

3 LARGE CARROTS, DICED

1 TBSP GARLIC, MINCED

3 CUPS ROTISSERIE CHICKEN, SHREDDED

32 OUNCES CHICKEN STOCK

2 LARGE POTATOES, CUBED

1 TBSP BETTER THAN BOUILLON PASTE, CHICKEN FLAVOR

1 TSP DRIED THYME

1 BAY LEAF

1 CUP FROZEN PEAS

1 CUP FROZEN CORN

6 OUNCES (HALF BAG) BROAD EGG NOODLES

SALT AND PEPPER TO TASTE, PARSLEY, CHOPPED FOR TOPPING

PREPARATION

1. Add olive oil, onion, celery, and carrots to a large pot.

2. Cook for 5 minutes, add garlic and cook for another minute.

3. Add shredded chicken, chicken stock, potatoes, Better Than Bouillon paste, thyme, bay leaf, salt, and pepper. Bring to a boil.

4. Add the frozen corn and peas and bring back to a boil.

5. Add the egg noodles and cook for 10 minutes.

6. Reduce to a simmer before adding the egg noodles.

7. Move the soup to a serving bowl, top with chopped parsley.

Enjoy.

Soups are one of my favorite dishes to make, especially when cold weather starts to set in here in New England. Whenever I ask my daughter what kind of soup she wants, the answer is always the same: chicken noodle. It's her comfort in a bowl; rich broth, tender chicken, veggies and plenty of noodles. Simple, classic, and always made with love for my girl.

Split Pea & Ham Soup

PREPARATION

1. Put the ham bone and 5 cups of water in a large pot and simmer for 1 hour.

2. In a second large pot, add olive oil over medium heat, add the onions and sauté for 3 minutes. Add the garlic and sauté for another minute.

3. Take the ham bone out of the water and set aside, then add the liquid from that pot to the pot with onions and garlic.

4. Add vegetable broth, ham bone, split peas, carrots, potatoes, bay leaf, thyme, and salt and pepper to taste (be careful with the salt and taste test before adding more).

5. Cover and let simmer over low heat for 60-80 minutes. Stir the soup every half hour or so and add water as needed.

6. Take the ham bone out of the soup, pull all the meat off the bone, and add it to the soup.

7. Add more leftover ham if there wasn't enough meat on the bone.

8. Discard the bay leaf.

    Enjoy!

INGREDIENTS

1 MEDIUM TO LARGE HAM BONE WITH SOME MEAT STILL ON THE BONE

5 CUPS WATER

1 TBSP OLIVE OIL

1 TBSP SWEET ONION, MINCED

1 TSP GARLIC, MINCED

4 CUPS VEGETABLE STOCK

1 16-OUNCE BAG DRIED SPLIT PEAS, SORTED, RINSED AND DRAINED

2 MEDIUM CARROTS, PEELED AND DICED

2 SMALL POTATOES, PEELED AND DICED

1 BAY LEAF

½ TSP THYME

SALT AND PEPPER TO TASTE

Turkey, Mushroom, and Barley Soup

Ingredients

2 TBSP OLIVE OIL

1 ONION, DICED

3 CARROTS, CHOPPED

3 CELERY STALKS, CHOPPED

8 OUNCES MUSHROOMS, CHOPPED

32 OUNCES LOW SODIUM CHICKEN BROTH

1 LB. COOKED AND CHOPPED TURKEY BREAST

2 BAY LEAVES

½ TSP THYME

1 TSP BETTER THAN BOULLION (CHICKEN)

1 CUP BARLEY

SALT AND PEPPER TO TASTE

Preparation

1. In a Dutch oven, heat the olive oil over medium heat.
2. Add the onion, carrots, and celery, and cook for 3 to 5 minutes.
3. Add the mushrooms and cook for 2 minutes.
4. Add chicken broth, turkey (cooked and chopped), bay leaves, thyme, and better than boullion.
5. Add salt and pepper to taste.
6. Simmer for 20 minutes.
7. Add barley, turn off the heat, and let sit for 10 to 15 minutes.

Enjoy!

Pumpkin, Kale, and Quinoa Soup

PREPARATION

1. Cook quinoa according to the instructions on the package.

2. In a large saucepan over medium heat, add 1 TBSP of olive oil, shallots, and half of the garlic. Cook for 3 minutes or until translucent.

3. Add pumpkin puree, vegetable stock, coconut milk, maple syrup, and all seasonings.

4. Continue to cook over low heat while you sauté the kale.

5. In a skillet, add 1 TBSP olive oil, the rest of the garlic, and chopped kale. Sauté kale until wilted.

6. Top the soup with the sautéed kale and cooked quinoa. Serve.

   Enjoy!

INGREDIENTS

1 CUP OF QUINOA

2 TBSP OLIVE OIL

2 SHALLOTS, DICED

2 TBSP GARLIC, MINCED

2-¼ CUPS PUMPKIN PUREE

2 CUPS VEGETABLE STOCK

1 CUP LIGHT COCONUT MILK

3 TBSP MAPLE SYRUP

1 BAG CHOPPED KALE

¼ TSP EACH: SALT, PEPPER, CINNAMON, AND NUTMEG

Roasted Eggplant and Red Pepper Soup

INGREDIENTS

- **1** CUP QUINOA
- **2** RED BELL PEPPERS
- **1** EGGPLANT
- **¼** CUP OLIVE OIL
- **1** ONION, CHOPPED
- **4** CLOVES GARLIC, MINCED
- **2** SMALL ZUCCHINI, CUBED
- **1** 14-OUNCE CAN DICED TOMATO
- **32** OUNCES VEGETABLE BROTH
- SALT AND PEPPER TO TASTE
- **3** SPRIGS FRESH ROSEMARY

PREPARATION

1. Preheat oven to 400°F. Cook quinoa as instructed on the package.

2. Leave red peppers whole, drizzle with olive oil, and sprinkle with salt.

3. Cut the eggplant in half, drizzle it with olive oil, and sprinkle with salt. Lay cut side down on top of 1 sprig of rosemary. Poke the skin of the eggplant with a fork. Roast both eggplant and peppers for 50 minutes.

4. Let cool, then peel the skin from the peppers and the eggplant. Pull the seeds from the red peppers. Cut peppers and eggplant into cubes.

5. In a Dutch oven, add 2 TBSP olive oil; sauté chopped onions and garlic, then add the roasted eggplant, roasted red peppers, zucchini, and diced tomatoes.

6. Add vegetable broth, cooked quinoa, 2 sprigs of fresh rosemary, and salt and pepper to taste.

7. Cook all together on low heat for 30 minutes.

Enjoy!

ALWAYS ALLIE

Sweet Potato and Ground Turkey Chili

INGREDIENTS

1 LB. GROUND TURKEY

1 ONION, CHOPPED

3 SWEET POTATOES, CUBED AND PEELED

1 RED BELL PEPPER, CHOPPED

1 28-OUNCE CAN CRUSHED TOMATO

1 8-OUNCE CAN TOMATO SAUCE

2 CUPS CHICKEN BONE BROTH

1 TBSP GARLIC, MINCED

1 TBSP CUMIN

1 TSP CHILI POWDER

½ TSP CINNAMON

2 8-OUNCE CANS BLACK BEANS, RINSED AND DRAINED

2 CUPS FROZEN CORN

2 TBSP OLIVE OIL

SALT AND PEPPER

PREPARATION

1. **In a Dutch oven, heat olive oil over medium heat. Cook the ground turkey until completely cooked.**

   Add onions and sweet potatoes; cook for about 3 minutes.

2. **Add crushed tomatoes, tomato sauce, bone broth, garlic, and all spices.**

3. **Reduce heat and simmer for about half an hour or until sweet potatoes become soft.**

4. **Stir often.**

5. **Add corn and black beans and cook for about 5 additional minutes.**

6. **Serve hot with a delish cornbread
   (see page 190 for recipe).**

   Enjoy!

RECIPE BOOK

Chicken and White Bean Chili

Ingredients

2 tbsp olive oil

1 onion, diced

7 cups chicken broth

3 15-ounce cans of Great Northern beans, rinsed and drained, 1 can mashed

4 cloves garlic, minced

1 4-ounce can, green chilis

1-¼ lb. cooked chicken breast, shredded

1 cup cilantro leaves, chopped

1 tsp cumin

1 tsp oregano

1 tsp paprika

1 tsp chili powder

¼ tsp black pepper

¼ tsp salt

Preparation

1. In a large stockpot, add olive oil and sauté the onions until they are soft.

2. Add chicken broth, mashed beans, whole beans, garlic, and chilis; bring to a boil.

3. Add chicken, ½ of the chopped cilantro, and all seasonings (cumin, oregano, paprika, chili powder, black pepper, and salt). Reduce heat to medium and let simmer.

4. Let the chili simmer at least another 30 minutes; the longer, the better.

5. Before serving, add the rest of the cilantro.

Enjoy!

RECIPES IN THIS SECTION

- Stuffed Bell Peppers
- Ham and Broccoli Quiche
- Stuffed Butternut Squash
- Butternut Squash Spinach Lasagna Rolls
- Coconut Curry Shrimp with Cilantro Lime Rice
- Ground Turkey and Sweet Potato Skillet
- Chicken Pot Pie
- Cajun Shrimp Foils
- Pan Seared Scallops
- Easy Mushroom Risotto
- Chicken Tacos
- Braised Beef Short Ribs
- Beef Stew
- Canadian Meat Pie (Tourtière)
- Chicken Cacciatore
- Shrimp, Sausage and Rice Skillet
- Sweet Potato and Black Bean Burger

Mains

> "I cook with wine, and sometimes I add it to the food. ...W.C. Fields

Stuffed Bell Peppers

PREPARATION

1. Preheat oven to 350.

2. Cook the rice according to the package directions.

3. Add the ground beef and salt and pepper to taste to the pan; cook the ground beef until the meat is no longer pink, remove the meat from the pan, and discard the rendered fat.

4. Cut the tops off each bell pepper, remove the stems, deseed, and chop.

5. Add cooked beef back into the pan, along with chopped onion, chopped bell pepper tops, and garlic; cook until the pepper and onions are soft.

6. Bring a large pot of water to a boil. Add the peppers to the boiling water for 10 minutes, then remove and place the peppers in a baking dish.

7. Add pasta sauce, Italian seasoning, and cooked rice to the meat and pepper mixture.

8. Combine well and stuff the mixture in each pepper.

9. Top each pepper with shredded cheese. Bake for 20 minutes.

   Enjoy!

INGREDIENTS

1 CUP RICE

2 TBSP OLIVE OIL

1 LB. GROUND BEEF

4 MEDIUM-SIZED BELL PEPPERS (USE ANY COLOR)

1 LARGE, SWEET ONION, CHOPPED

1 TBSP GARLIC, MINCED

25-OUNCE JAR PASTA SAUCE

1 TSP ITALIAN SEASONING

1 CUP SHREDDED ITALIAN CHEESE

SALT AND PEPPER TO TASTE

Ham and Broccoli Quiche

INGREDIENTS

1 TBSP OLIVE OIL

7-OUNCE HAM STEAK, CUBED

1 CUP FROZEN BROCCOLI, CHOPPED

1 LARGE ONION, CHOPPED

1 TBSP MINCED GARLIC

1 LARGE CARROT, SHREDDED

1 PIE CRUST

6 LARGE EGGS

½ CUP MILK

½ TSP DRY MUSTARD

1 TSP SALT

½ TSP PEPPER

½ CUP SHARP SHREDDED CHEESE

PREPARATION

1. Preheat oven to 375°F.

2. Over medium heat, place oil, ham, broccoli, onions, and garlic in a large pan, and sauté until onions are soft, then add shredded carrots and cook for 1 minute.

3. Par-bake the pie crust for 15 minutes.

4. In a bowl, whisk together eggs, milk, dry mustard, salt, and pepper.

5. Once mixed together, add cheese and stir.

6. Once the pie crust is par-baked, add the ham and broccoli mixture, then pour the egg and cheese mixture over, and use a fork to move the ingredients around so they are well incorporated.

7. Bake for 30 to 40 minutes or until the center has set.

   Enjoy!

Stuffed Butternut Squash

PREPARATION

1. Preheat oven to 400°F. Slice the butternut squash in half lengthwise. Using a spoon, scoop out the seeds and strands. Discard.

2. Place parchment paper on a baking sheet. Rub 2 TBSP of olive oil all over the squash and season with salt and pepper. Place the squash, cut side down, and roast for 20 minutes. Remove from oven, turn squash over; roast another 20 minutes.

3. While the squash is roasting, prepare stuffing. In a large skillet, add 1 TBSP olive oil and onion, and sauté on medium heat for 2 minutes.

4. Add sausage, minced garlic, sage. Sauté until the sausage is cooked through. Add fresh chopped spinach, cook to wilt spinach. Add chopped cranberries and pecans. Salt and pepper to taste.

5. Remove roasted squash from oven. Scoop out the inside of the squash with a spoon, leaving about a 1-inch border of squash.

6. Add the scooped squash to the stuffing mixture and mix well. Transfer the stuffing equally to each half of the squash.

7. Place squash back in oven for 10 minutes; remove then serve.

   Enjoy!

INGREDIENTS

1 LARGE BUTTERNUT SQUASH

3 TBSP OLIVE OIL

1 ONION, DICED

16-OUNCE PACKAGE OF JIMMY DEAN SAUSAGE

1 TBSP GARLIC, MINCED

1 TBSP FRESH SAGE

5 OUNCES FRESH BABY SPINACH, CHOPPED

½ CUP DRIED CRANBERRIES, CHOPPED

½ CUP PECANS, CHOPPED

SALT AND PEPPER

Butternut Squash and Spinach Lasagna Rolls

INGREDIENTS

9 LASAGNA NOODLES

1 LB. BUTTERNUT SQUASH, PEELED AND CUBED

1 TBSP OLIVE OIL

1 SHALLOT, MINCED

2 GARLIC CLOVES, MINCED

½ CUP PLUS 2 TBSP GRATED PARMESAN CHEESE

10 OUNCES FROZEN CHOPPED SPINACH, THAWED AND LIQUID SQUEEZED OUT

15 OZ RICOTTA CHEESE

1 LARGE EGG

½ CUP ITALIAN BLEND SHREDDED CHEESE

1 TBSP PARSLEY, MINCED

SALT AND PEPPER TO TASTE

PREPARATION

1. Preheat oven to 350. Cook lasagna noodles as directed on the packaging.

2. Cook butternut squash in salted boiling water until soft. Reserve 1 cup of the water. Strain the cooked butternut squash.

3. In a skillet, add olive oil, shallots, and garlic; sauté until soft.

4. Place cooked butternut squash, cooked shallots, garlic, 2 TBSP Parmesan cheese, and salt and pepper to taste into a bowl. Blend with an immersion blender until smooth, using reserved water, if needed.

5. In a separate medium bowl, mix together the egg, spinach, ricotta, and 1 cup of Parmesan cheese.

6. Ladle a layer of the butternut sauce on the bottom of a 12 x 9-inch dish.

7. Place a piece of parchment paper on the counter and lay out the lasagna noodles. Drizzle with a little olive oil so the slices do not stick together.

8. Spread ricotta mixture evenly over each lasagna noodle. Carefully roll noodles and place seam-side down in the baking dish. Ladle remaining butternut sauce over the rolls and sprinkle the Italian blend shredded cheese over the top.

9. Bake covered with foil for 40 minutes. Top with parsley, serve, and enjoy.

>> *While visiting Belize, we stumbled upon a beachfront restaurant serving incredible coconut curry shrimp with cilantro lime rice. From the first bite, I wanted to recreate it at home. The flavors were bold and comforting, with the right balance of spice, creaminess, and citrus. I went back to have it again. Back home, I nailed a version that comes close to that unforgettable meal. It is a favorite and brings back memories of that breezy Belizean beach.*

ALWAYS ALLIE

Coconut Curry Shrimp with Cilantro Lime Rice

PREPARATION

1. Rice: Combine rice, coconut milk, water, lime juice, lime zest, cilantro, and salt and pepper to taste in a pot.

2. Cook for 15-20 minutes, until tender.

3. Shrimp: In a large skillet over medium heat, add 1 TBSP olive oil, onion, peppers, carrots, garlic, and salt and pepper to taste.

4. Sauté for 10 minutes. Add coconut milk; let sit on low heat while shrimp cooks.

5. In a separate pan over low heat, add 1 TBSP olive oil, raw shrimp, and curry powder.

6. Cook shrimp halfway through on low heat.

7. Once the shrimp is halfway cooked, add peppers, onions, carrots, lime juice, and cilantro to the skillet and cook for an additional 5 minutes.

8. Serve over rice.

   Enjoy!

INGREDIENTS

2 TBSP OLIVE OIL

1 SWEET ONION, THINLY SLICED

2 RED BELL PEPPERS, THINLY SLICED

1 PACKAGE MATCHSTICK CARROTS

1 CLOVE GARLIC, MINCED OR CRUSHED

1 CAN LIGHT COCONUT MILK

1 LB. RAW SHRIMP, PEELED AND DEVEINED

2 TBSP CURRY POWDER

1 LIME, JUICED

1 TBSP CILANTRO, CHOPPED

SALT AND PEPPER TO TASTE

For Cilantro Lime Rice:

1 CUP JASMINE RICE

1 CUP LIGHT COCONUT MILK

1 CUP WATER

1 LIME, JUICED AND ZESTED

1 TBSP CILANTRO, CHOPPED

SALT AND PEPPER TO TASTE

Ground Turkey and Sweet Potato Skillet

INGREDIENTS

2 TBSP OLIVE OIL

1 LB. GROUND TURKEY

1 ONION, CHOPPED

2 SWEET POTATOES, DICED

1 TBSP GARLIC, MINCED

1 TBSP GROUND CUMIN

1 PINCH OF RED PEPPER FLAKES

1 YELLOW BELL PEPPER, CHOPPED

1 CUP SHREDDED MOZZARELLA CHEESE

1 TBSP PARSLEY, CHOPPED

SALT AND PEPPER TO TASTE

PREPARATION

1. In a large cast-iron skillet, heat olive oil over medium heat.

2. Add turkey and onions, and while cooking, break the meat apart with a wooden spoon.

   Cook for 10 minutes.

3. Add sweet potatoes, garlic, cumin, red pepper flakes, and salt and pepper to taste and mix together.

4. Cover and cook for 10 minutes. stirring every few minutes.

5. Add the yellow bell peppers and cook for another 10 minutes, stirring every few minutes.

6. Add shredded mozzarella, then top with chopped parsley.

7. Put a lid on and remove from the heat, allowing the cheese to melt.

   Enjoy.

ALWAYS ALLIE

Twenty or so years ago, my husband and I set out to make the perfect chicken pot pie—and we did. After years of searching, tasting and fine-tuning, this golden, flaky, delicious masterpiece has become ours and our daughter's absolute favorite dish. It is comfort food at its finest, made with love and memories in every bite.

ALWAYS ALLIE

Chicken Pot Pie

PREPARATION

1. Preheat oven to 350°F.

2. Melt butter in a large skillet, cook onion until tender, stir in celery and carrots; cook for 2 minutes.

3. Stir in flour; cook for 2 minutes.

4. Add chicken stock and the Better Than Bouillon; bring to a simmer.

5. Add potatoes; simmer until tender.

6. Stir in chicken, parsley, and peas.

7. Blind-bake the bottom pie crust for 15 minutes.

8. Pour the mixture into the prepared pie crust.

9. Top with second pie crust; brush with lightly beaten egg.

10. Bake for 30 minutes or until the crust is golden brown.

11. Let the pie cool for 15 minutes. Serve with cranberry sauce.

    Enjoy!

INGREDIENTS

2 TBSP BUTTER

1 ONION, CHOPPED

2 CARROTS, DICED

2 CELERY STALKS, DICED

4 TBSP FLOUR

4 CUPS CHICKEN STOCK

2 POTATOES, PEELED AND DICED

2 CUPS SHREDDED CHICKEN

2 TBSP CHOPPED PARSLEY

½ CUP THAWED FROZEN PEAS

2 PREPARED REFRIGERATED PIE CRUSTS

1 EGG, LIGHTLY BEATEN

1 TBSP CHICKEN FLAVORED BETTER THAN BOUILLON

SALT AND PEPPER TO TASTE

Cajun Shrimp Foils

INGREDIENTS

2 LBS. BABY YELLOW POTATOES

5 EARS SWEET CORN ON THE COB, CUT INTO 2-3-INCH PIECES

1 LB. RAW SHRIMP

1 LB. ANDOUILLE SAUSAGE

2 TBSP OLIVE OIL

2 TBSP CAJUN SEASONING (OLD BAY)

2 CLOVES GARLIC, MINCED

2 TBSP PARSLEY

8 TBSP SALTED BUTTER, CUBED

SALT AND PEPPER TO TASTE

PREPARATION

1. Bring a large pot of water to boil. Add the corn and baby yellow potatoes and boil for 10 minutes.
2. Drain and place in a large bowl.
3. To a large bowl, add the shrimp, sausage, oil, and Old Bay seasoning. Add salt and pepper to taste.
4. Mix together until everything is coated.
5. To assemble, tear four pieces of foil and lay them flat.
6. Place the mixture in the center of the foil, making it as even as possible.
7. Place an even amount of butter on top of the mixture on each piece of foil. Sprinkle parsley on top of each foil pouch.
8. Place another piece of foil on top, curl it up, and pinch the sides of the foil together.
9. Preheat the grill to 400°F.
10. Add the packets to the grill and cook for fifteen minutes, flipping halfway through.
11. Carefully open the packets, and serve.

    Enjoy!

Pan Seared Scallops

PREPARATION

1. Heat a cast-iron skillet over medium heat.

2. Pat scallops dry with a paper towel. Sprinkle the scallops with salt and pepper.

3. When the pan is hot, add olive oil and butter. Place your scallops in the pan with enough room between them so they don't steam each other.

4. Cook the scallops for two minutes, making sure not to overcook. Flip the scallops over with a pair of tongs and cook for another two minutes.

5. Remove and serve.

6. These are great paired with Mushroom Risotto. Just turn the page for the recipe.

    Enjoy!

INGREDIENTS

1 LB. WILD-CAUGHT SCALLOPS

1 TBSP OLIVE OIL

2 TBSP BUTTER

SALT AND PEPPER TO TASTE

RECIPE BOOK

Easy Mushroom Risotto

PREPARATION

1. Add 2 TBSP of olive oil to a large pan over medium heat.
2. Add chopped mushrooms and garlic to pan and cook until soft, about 5 minutes.
3. Turn the heat off and set aside.
4. Add 2 TBSP of olive oil to a large saucepan over medium heat.
5. Add shallots and cook for 1 minute. Add the rice, stirring constantly until it turns a golden color, about 3 minutes.
6. Pour wine over the rice and stir constantly until the wine is absorbed. Next, add ½ cup of broth to rice, cook and stir until the broth is absorbed.
7. Continue this step by adding ½ cup of the remaining broth at a time, cooking and stirring constantly until the rice is al dente.
8. This takes around 20 minutes.
9. Remove from heat. Stir in cooked mushrooms, butter, chives, and Parmesan cheese.
10. Season with salt and pepper to taste. Serve right away.

    Enjoy!

INGREDIENTS

- 6 CUPS CHICKEN BROTH
- 4 TBSP OLIVE OIL
- 1 LB. SHITAKE MUSHROOMS, CHOPPED
- 1 LB. BABY PORTOBELLO MUSHROOMS, CHOPPED
- 2 TBSP GARLIC, MINCED
- 2 SHALLOTS, FINELY DICED
- 1 ½ CUPS ARBORIO RICE
- ½ CUP WHITE WINE
- 4 TBSP BUTTER
- 3 TBSP CHIVES, CHOPPED
- 1/3 CUP PARMESAN CHEESE, GRATED
- SALT AND PEPPER TO TASTE

Chicken Tacos

INGREDIENTS

2 TBSP OLIVE OIL

2 LBS. FRESH CHICKEN STRIPS OR TENDERS

2 TSP CHILI POWDER

2 TSP GROUND CUMIN

1 TSP GARLIC POWDER

1 TSP DRIED OREGANO

½ TSP PAPRIKA

SALT AND PEPPER TO TASTE

TORTILLAS, WARMED

INGREDIENTS FOR TOPPINGS

DICED TOMATOES

SALSA

SHREDDED CHEESE

SOUR CREAM

GUACAMOLE
(RECIPE IS ON PAGE 54)

LIME WEDGES

PREPARATION

1. Heat olive oil in a large skillet over medium heat.

2. Place chicken strips in a skillet and season with salt and pepper to taste.

3. Cook until the meat is no longer pink in the middle, about 10 minutes.

4. Remove the chicken from the skillet and rough chop the chicken.

5. Place the chopped chicken back in the skillet, add the spices, and stir until the chicken is well-coated.

6. You can add a small amount of oil or water if needed.

7. Build tacos in warm tortillas with chicken, tomatoes, salsa, shredded cheese, sour cream, guacamole, and lime wedges.

Enjoy!

Braised Beef Short Ribs

Ingredients

5 LBS. BONE-IN BEEF SHORT RIBS

3 TBSP OLIVE OIL

2 ONIONS, CHOPPED

3 CARROTS, CUT INTO LARGE PIECES

3 CELERY STALKS, CHOPPED

3 TBSP ALL-PURPOSE FLOUR

3 TBSP TOMATO PASTE

1 BOTTLE OF CABERNET SAUVIGNON

4 SPRIGS EACH (ROSEMARY, THYME, OREGANO) BUNDLE IN CHEESECLOTH

1 TBSP GARLIC, CRUSHED

4 CUPS OF BEEF BONE BROTH

5 LBS. POTATOES, COOKED AND MASHED

SALT AND PEPPER TO TASTE

Preparation

1. Preheat oven to 350°F. Season the short ribs with salt and pepper. Heat oil in a large Dutch oven over medium-high heat. In batches, brown the short ribs on all sides. Transfer the short ribs to a plate.

2. Add onions, carrots, and celery to the same pot and cook over medium heat, stirring often, until onions are browned, about 5 minutes.

3. Add flour and tomato paste; cook, stirring constantly, until well combined and deep red, 2-3 minutes.

4. Stir in the wine and scrape the bottom of the pot to combine all the goodness.

5. Add the short ribs with all juices. Bring to a boil; lower heat and simmer until wine is reduced, about 25 minutes.

6. Add all herbs and garlic to the pot. Stir in the stock. Bring to a boil, cover, and transfer to the oven. Cook for 2 hours, until ribs are tender.

7. Serve over mashed potatoes.

   Enjoy!

» Braised beef short ribs is one of my favorite dishes for as long as I can remember. I can't recall the first time I had them, but I know from the first bite, I wanted to recreate them at home. My version ia a go-to recipe and truly my favorite dish to make. It is deeply satisfying, filled with rich, tender meat, and savory flavors. It brings comfort to whoever's at the table. I love making it for people I care about and watching them take the first bite, seeing their eyes light up, hearing their sounds of delight. The joy they feel fills me up, too.

» *Beef stew takes me back to my childhood. My mother made it on Sundays during the winter, and the smell filled the house while football played in the background. It was hearty, warm, and felt like a hug in a bowl. I created my version over the years. Mine still brings the same sense of comfort and nostalgia. It's a favorite winter dish in our home, carrying on the tradition in its way.*

Beef Stew

PREPARATION

1. Preheat oven to 325°F and set a rack in the lower position.

2. Put salt, pepper, and flour on a plate, then place the meat in the mixture and coat all pieces of beef.

3. Heat 1 TBSP of olive oil in a Dutch oven, add 1/3 of the beef and brown; once browned, place the browned meat in a dish on the side.

4. Repeat this step 3 times.

5. Add onions, garlic, balsamic vinegar, and wine.

6. Cook for 5 minutes, stirring up bits on the bottom with a wooden spoon.

7. Add tomato sauce, diced tomatoes, the browned beef with the juices, beef broth, bay leaf, rosemary, thyme, and sugar, and stir well.

8. Add carrots and potatoes, cover, and transfer to the oven for 2-3 hours.

9. Take out of the oven and let sit for 30 minutes.

10. Take out the bay leaf and rosemary sprigs and discard.

11. Serve warm with bread or rolls.

    Enjoy!

INGREDIENTS

2 TBSP SALT

1 TBSP PEPPER

¼ CUP FLOUR

3 LBS. BONELESS BEEF CHUCK ROAST (WELL MARBLED), CUT INTO 1-INCH PIECES

3 TBSP OLIVE OIL

1 SWEET ONION, CHOPPED

2 TBSP GARLIC, SMASHED

2 TBSP BALSAMIC VINEGAR

2 CUPS CABERNET SAUVIGNON RED WINE

14-OUNCE CAN TOMATO SAUCE

14-OUNCE CAN DICED TOMATOES

4 CUPS BEEF BROTH

1 BAY LEAF

4 SPRIGS OF ROSEMARY

½ TSP DRIED THYME

1 TBSP SUGAR

4 LARGE CARROTS, CUT INTO BIG CHUNKS

1 LB. POTATOES, CUT INTO BIG CHUNKS

RECIPE BOOK

Canadian Meat Pie (Tourtière)

INGREDIENTS

2 LARGE POTATOES, PEELED AND CHOPPED

1 LB. GROUND PORK

1 LB. GROUND BEEF

1 ONION, CHOPPED

1 TBSP GARLIC, MINCED

½ TSP POULTRY SEASONING

¼ TSP CINNAMON, NUTMEG, GROUND CLOVE, SALT, AND BLACK PEPPER

2 PREMADE REFRIGERATED PIE CRUSTS

1 LARGE EGG, BEATEN

PREPARATION

1. Preheat oven to 375°F.

2. Boil the potatoes until they are soft, then drain all the water. Mash the potatoes and set them aside (do not add any butter or milk when mashing). If the potatoes are dry, add a little water.

3. In a large skillet, cook the pork, ground beef, onion, and garlic; drain the rendered fat.

4. Mix the meat mixture with the mashed potatoes and all the spices.

5. Place one pie crust in the pie plate and blind-bake for 15 minutes.

6. Add the mixture to the prepared pie crust and spread evenly. Cover with the top crust.

7. Brush with beaten egg. Cut slits into the crust to steam vent. Bake for 45 minutes. Serve with cranberry sauce.

   Enjoy!

> Tourtière is a classic French Canadian meat pie that runs deep in my mom's family and my husband's father's family. It's not the most glamorous dish on the table, but it's one of the best I've ever made. Rich, savory, and full of comforting spices, it's a true taste of heritage. I love serving it to people who think they won't like it. I say, "Try a little piece," and they're always shocked at how delicious it is. Pairing with a spoonful of cranberry sauce, rounds out the teaste with a bright touch of sweetness.

Jambalaya

INGREDIENTS

2 TBSP OLIVE OIL

1 ONION, DICED

2 CELERY STALKS, CHOPPED

1 LARGE GREEN BELL PEPPER, CORED, SEEDED, AND CHOPPED

12-OUNCES ANDOUILLE SAUSAGE OR KIELBASA, SLICED INTO ½-INCH PIECES

1 14-OUNCE CAN DICED TOMATOES

1 14-OUNCE CAN CRUSHED TOMATO

1 14-OUNCE CAN ARTICHOKES, CHOPPED

1 LB. CHICKEN BREAST, BOILED AND SHREDDED

32-OUNCES LOW SODIUM CHICKEN BROTH

1 CUP UNCOOKED RICE

2 BAY LEAVES

1 TBSP CAJUN SEASONING

1 16-OUNCE. BAG FROZEN SHRIMP, WILD-CAUGHT

2 CLOVES GARLIC, MINCED

1 TSP SMOKED HOT PEPPER SAUCE

SALT AND PEPPER TO TASTE

PREPARATION

1. In a Dutch oven heat olive oil over medium heat. Sauté onion, celery, and bell pepper; stir constantly for 3 to 5 minutes.

2. Add the kielbasa (or andouille sausage) and cook for 3 minutes.

3. Stir in both cans of tomatoes and the artichokes.

4. Add chicken, chicken broth, rice, bay leaves, Cajun seasoning, and salt and pepper to taste.

5. Simmer and stir constantly for 25 minutes or until rice is tender.

6. Add shrimp and smoked hot sauce; simmer for 5 minutes.

Enjoy!

RECIPE BOOK

Chicken Cacciatore

INGREDIENTS

6–8 BONELESS, SKINLESS CHICKEN THIGHS

3 TBSP OLIVE OIL

1 LARGE ONION, CHOPPED

2 TBSP GARLIC, MINCED

10 OUNCES MUSHROOMS, SLICED

1 LARGE CARROT, PEELED AND SLICED

1 YELLOW BELL PEPPER, DICED

1 RED BELL PEPPER, DICED

1 28-OUNCE CAN CRUSHED TOMATOES

2 TBSP TOMATO PASTE

7 OUNCES ROMA TOMATOES

1 CUP RED WINE

1 TSP EACH FRESH PARSLEY, BASIL, THYME, AND OREGANO, CHOPPED

1 TBSP SUGAR

½ TSP RED PEPPER FLAKES

1 CAN PITTED MEDIUM BLACK OLIVES

SALT AND PEPPER TO TASTE

PREPARATION

1. Season chicken thighs with salt and pepper.

2. Heat 2 TBSP olive oil in a large skillet, add chicken, and cook for 8 minutes on each side (working in batches if needed).

3. Once the chicken is cooked, transfer it to a plate and set aside.

4. Add the remaining olive oil to the skillet along with the onion, garlic, mushrooms, carrots, and bell peppers and cook.

5. Scrape up the browned bits on the bottom of the pan; cook until tender.

6. Add all cans of tomatoes, including juices, tomato paste, wine, parsley, basil, thyme, oregano, sugar, red pepper flakes, and salt and pepper to taste.

7. Return the chicken to the pan, add black olives, and simmer uncovered until the sauce reduces and the chicken is cooked through.

8. Serve over white rice or any small pasta

Enjoy!

> I can't resist calling this dish Chicken Catch-a-Corey because my husband's name is Corey. It's classic comfort food, slowly simmered with tender chicken, peppers, onions, and a rich tomato sauce. Around here, when I say I'm making "Chicken Catch-a-Corey," it always gets a laugh, and I have a hard time calling this dish by its real name.

Shrimp, Sausage, and Rice Skillet

PREPARATION

1. Add water to the saucepan, bring to a boil and cook rice, following instructions on the package.
2. Heat olive oil in a large skillet over medium heat.
3. Clean shrimp, season with Old Bay seasoning.
4. Add shrimp and cook until opaque. Remove and set aside.
5. Cook diced onion and bell peppers in juices from shrimp for 10 minutes.
6. Add sausage and zucchini; cook for 15 minutes.
7. Add shrimp back into the skillet, add garlic, and cook everything for 5 minutes.
8. Pour in vegetarian stock and cooked rice and mix everything together.
9. Add paprika, salt, and pepper to the mixture in the skillet.

    Enjoy!

INGREDIENTS

1 CUP JASMINE RICE

OLIVE OIL

1 16-OUNCE BAG SHRIMP (PEELED AND DEVEINED)

2 TSP OLD BAY SEASONING

1 MEDIUM ONION, DICED

1 GREEN BELL PEPPER, DICED

1 RED BELL PEPPER, DICED

13 OUNCES TURKEY SMOKED SAUSAGE

1 ZUCCHINI, CHOPPED

2 CLOVES GARLIC, MINCED

¼ CUP VEGETARIAN STOCK

¼ TSP SMOKED PAPRIKA

SALT AND PEPPER TO TASTE

Sweet Potato and Black Bean Burger

INGREDIENTS

- 2 LARGE SWEET POTATOES = 2 CUPS PEELED AND DICED
- 1 TBSP OLIVE OIL
- 14-OUNCE OF CAN BLACK BEANS, RINSED AND DRAINED
- 1 ½ CUPS QUINOA OR BROWN RICE
- 1 CUP OF GLUTEN-FREE BREADCRUMBS
- 1 EGG
- ¼ CUP CHOPPED CILANTRO LEAVES
- 1 TBSP CUMIN
- 1 TSP CHILI POWDER
- 1 TSP LIME JUICE
- ½ TSP OREGANO
- ½ TSP GARLIC SALT
- SALT AND PEPPER TO TASTE

TOPPING IDEAS: LETTUCE, TOMATO, PICKLES, AND AVOCADO

PREPARATION

1. Preheat oven to 400°F.
2. Peel and dice the sweet potatoes, toss with 1 TBSP olive oil and a pinch of salt and pepper. Add sweet potatoes to a baking pan and roast for 30-40 minutes until soft.
3. While the sweet potatoes are roasting, make the rice or quinoa, and set aside.
4. Once sweet potatoes are roasted, mash them with fork or potato masher and mix remaining ingredients together (excluding toppings), and place in the fridge for 15-20 minutes to cool.
5. Preheat a non-stick pan (preferably cast iron) to medium heat. Lightly oil with olive oil or cooking spray.
6. Scoop out 1/2 cup of the mixture and form into a patty. Place patty into the pre-heated pan, cook for 4-5 minutes per side until crispy and lightly browned.
7. Place on a toasted bun and serve with toppings of choice.

Enjoy!

RECIPES IN THIS SECTION

- But You Ain't Ever Had My Cornbread
- Focaccia Bread
- Zucchini Chocolate Chip Bread
- Chocolate Chip Banana Bread
- Chocolate Peppermint Cookies
- Red Velvet Cupcakes with Cream Cheese Frosting
- Pumpkin Bundt Cake
- Maple-Pecan Glaze
- Apple Crisp
- Pistachio Cake with Icing
- Pumpkin Pie
- Mulled Apple Cider
- Espresso Martini

Breads, Desserts, and Drinks

> **My secret Ingredient is love.**

Cornbread in a cast-iron skillet was a true staple in our house growing up; it's something Mamaw or Dad would whip up regularly, and you could only find cornbread like that in the South. Golden, crispy on the edges, tender in the middle, and full of that unmistakable home-cooked flavor. After moving to New England, I realized just how hard it is to find the right cornmeal-to-flour ratio up here. So, I started making my own mixture with cornmeal, self-rising flour, and the not-so-secret but essential ingredient, bacon grease. That's the soul of Southern cornbread, and every time I make it, it tastes like home.

But You Ain't Ever Had My Cornbread

PREPARATION

1. Preheat oven to 425°F. Place the bacon grease in a cast-iron skillet, and place in the oven while preheating.

2. In a large bowl, mix the cornmeal, flour, sugar, baking powder, and salt.

3. Whisk the eggs, buttermilk, and melted butter in a separate bowl.

4. Pour the wet ingredients into the dry ingredients and stir until well mixed. This mixture will look a little lumpy.

5. Remove the skillet from the oven; carefully swirl the melted bacon grease all around the bottom and sides of the skillet. Pour batter into hot skillet; the batter will start to bubble and sizzle. This is what makes the crispy edges.

6. Bake until center is firm, 20 to 25 minutes.

7. Remove cornbread from the skillet immediately and let cool for 10 to 15 minutes.

8. Slice, serve, and enjoy!

INGREDIENTS

2 TBSP BACON GREASE

1-½ CUPS CORNMEAL

½ CUP SELF-RISING FLOUR

½ CUP SUGAR

1 TSP BAKING POWDER

½ TSP SALT

1-½ CUPS BUTTERMILK

2 LARGE EGGS

2 TBSP BUTTER, MELTED

Focaccia Bread

INGREDIENTS

500 G WHITE BREAD FLOUR

420 ML WARM WATER

1 TBSP OLIVE OIL

2 TSP SEA SALT

1 TSP INSTANT YEAST

1 TSP HONEY

PREPARATION

1. Place the flour in a large glass bowl.

2. Mix the water, olive oil, salt, yeast, and honey together in a separate bowl.

3. Once the water mixture is well incorporated, add it to the flour and stir until the flour is completely hydrated.

4. Scrape the sides of the bowl, and cover with a cloth for 10 minutes.

5. After 10 minutes, with wet hands, start to stretch and fold the dough over; repeat this process one more time.

6. After the second stretch and fold, place the dough smooth-side up in a dry bowl. Drizzle olive oil all over the dough, cover it with plastic wrap, and refrigerate overnight.

7. Line a baking pan with parchment paper and drizzle with olive oil. Place the dough on the pan and start pulling it up and folding it over four times. Turn the dough over so the smooth side is facing up. Cover with another pan and leave on the counter to proof for 2 hours.

8. Preheat the oven to 430°F. Oil your hands and start to dimple the dough with your fingers. Add any toppings you might like.

9. Bake for 18 to 20 minutes.

   Enjoy!

Zucchini chocolate chip bread holds a sweet spot in my kitchen thanks to my mother-in-law, Cindy. She's the one who first introduced me to zucchini bread. I was surprised by how moist and delicious it was. Of course, I couldn't resist putting my spin on it. I added chocolate chips, because why not? The result is a rich, tender bread with the right touch of sweetness. It's perfect for brunches, cozy mornings, or sitting on the counter for my daughter to grab a quick bite after school. It's become one of those simple, feel-good treats we always come back to.

Zucchini Chocolate Chip Bread

INGREDIENTS

3 LARGE EGGS

1-¾ CUPS SUGAR

2 CUPS GRATED ZUCCHINI, STRAINED

1 CUP UNSALTED BUTTER, MELTED

2 TSP VANILLA EXTRACT

3 CUPS ALL-PURPOSE FLOUR

2 TSP GROUND CINNAMON

1 TSP GROUND NUTMEG

½ TSP GROUND GINGER

1 TSP BAKING SODA

½ TSP BAKING POWDER

½ TSP SALT

1 CUP WALNUTS, CHOPPED

1 CUP CHOCOLATE CHIPS

PREPARATION

1. Preheat oven to 325°F. Generously grease a 9x13-inch glass baking dish.

2. In a large bowl, whisk eggs and sugar with a handheld mixer until well combined.

3. Add grated zucchini, melted butter, and vanilla extract; stir to combine.

4. Sift flour, cinnamon, nutmeg, ginger, baking soda, baking powder, and salt in another large bowl.

5. Stir dry ingredients into wet ingredients, 1/3 at a time, being careful not to overmix.

6. Fold in the nuts and chocolate chips.

7. Transfer batter into the greased 9x13-inch glass baking dish.

8. Bake for 30-40 minutes at 325°F, or until a toothpick inserted into the center comes out clean.

Enjoy!

Chocolate Chip Banana Bread

INGREDIENTS

1-½ cups unbleached all purpose flour

1 tsp baking soda

1 tsp cinnamon

½ tsp fine salt

2 large eggs, room temperature

1 tsp vanilla extract

½ cup unsalted butter, room temperature

1 cup sugar

3 ripe bananas, peeled and mashed

½ cup walnuts, chopped

½ cup dark chocolate chips

PREPARATION

1. Preheat oven to 350°F.

2. Sift flour, baking soda, cinnamon, and salt into a medium bowl; set aside.

3. Beat eggs and vanilla together in a small bowl; set aside.

4. Grease a 9x13-inch glass baking dish or spray with a baking spray.

5. With a standing mixer or hand-held mixer, cream the butter and sugar until light and fluffy.

6. Slowly pour the egg mixture into the butter/sugar mixture and continue mixing until combined. Then, add the bananas (the mixture will look a little funky, but that's supposed to be the case); remove it from the mixer.

7. With a rubber spatula, mix the flour mixture into the egg, banana, and sugar mixture until incorporated.

8. Fold in the walnuts and chocolate chips; transfer the batter to the prepared pan.

9. Bake for 30 minutes or until a toothpick inserted into the middle comes out clean.

Enjoy!

INGREDIENTS

CREAM CHESE FROSTING PREPARATION

16 OZ FULL-FAT CREAM CHEESE, ROOM TEMPERATURE

¾ CUP UNSALTED BUTTER, ROOM TEMPERATURE

5 CUPS CONFECTIONER'S SUGAR

1 ½ TSP PURE VANILLA EXTRACT

PINCH OF SALT

1. In a large bowl, use a handheld or stand mixer with whisk attachment, beat the cream cheese and butter on medium high speed until smooth.

2. Add confectioners' sugar, vanilla extract, and a pinch of salt. Beat on low to incorporate the sugar. Once mixed a bit, increase speed to high and beat until frosting is smooth and creamy. If it's too thin, add more confectioners' sugar. If it's too thick, add a tiny amount of water.

3. Pipe or spread frosting onto the cake or cupcakes after completely cooled.

   Enjoy!

ALWAYS ALLIE

Red Velvet Cupcakes and Cream Cheese Frosting

Ingredients

- 3 cups cake flour
- 1 tsp baking soda
- 2 tbsp unsweetened cocoa powder
- ½ tsp salt
- ½ cup unsalted butter, room temperature
- 2 cups sugar
- 1 cup vegetable oil
- 4 eggs, room temperature, and separated
- 1 tbsp pure vanilla extract
- 1 tsp white vinegar
- 1 cup buttermilk, room temperature
- Liquid red food coloring

Cupcake Preparation

1. Preheat oven to 350°F. Place 24 cupcake liners in cupcake pans.

2. In a large bowl, sift flour, baking soda, cocoa powder, and salt. Set aside.

3. Use handheld or stand mixer, beat butter and sugar on medium high until combined. Scrape the bowl's sides and bottom. Add the oil, egg yolks, vanilla extract, vinegar. Beat on high 2 minutes.

4. With the mixer on low speed, gradually add dry ingredients in 2-3 increments, alternate with the buttermilk. Beat in your desired amount of food coloring.

5. On high speed, beat 4 egg whites to fluffy peaks, about 3 minutes. Gently fold into the cake batter until silky, slightly thick.

6. Evenly distribute the batter into lined cupcake tins.

7. Bake for 15 to 20 minutes or until a toothpick inserted into the center comes out clean. Cool completely on a wire rack before frosting.

Enjoy!

Pumpkin Bundt Cake with Maple Pecan Glaze

INGREDIENTS

- 3 CUPS ALL-PURPOSE FLOUR
- 2 TSP BAKING POWDER
- 1 TSP BAKING SODA
- ½ TSP SALT
- 2 TSP GROUND CINNAMON
- ½ TSP GROUND NUTMEG
- ½ TSP GROUND GINGER
- ¼ TSP GROUND CLOVES OR ALLSPICE
- 8 OUNCES (2 STICKS) BUTTER
- 1 CUP SUGAR
- ¾ CUP PACKED BROWN SUGAR
- 5 LARGE EGGS
- 1 15-OUNCE CAN PUMPKIN
- 1 ½ TSP VANILLA

CAKE PREPARATION

1. Preheat the oven to 325°F. Spray the entire Bundt cake pan with baking spray.
2. In a medium bowl, combine flour, baking powder, soda, salt, and spices; set aside.
3. In a mixing bowl with an electric mixer, cream the butter and sugars until light and fluffy. Add the eggs, one at a time, beating well after each addition. Beat in the pumpkin and vanilla.
4. Slowly beat the dry ingredients into the batter. Continue mixing on medium speed until the batter is smooth and well-blended.
5. Spoon the cake batter into the prepared Bundt pan and bake for 55 to 60 minutes or until a wooden toothpick or cake tester comes out clean when inserted in the center.
6. Cool for 15 minutes in the pan on a rack; transfer to a serving plate and cool completely.
7. Apply Maple Pecan Glaze or dust with powdered sugar before serving.

Enjoy!

GLAZE PREPARATION

1. Combine butter, maple syrup, and cream in a small saucepan. Bring to a boil.

2. Boil 1 minute. Remove from heat and sift confectioners' sugar into the hot mixture. Whisk until smooth.

3. Let cool for 15 to 20 minutes, until slightly thickened. Stir in the finely chopped pecans, if using. Drizzle over cooled cake and enjoy.

INGREDIENTS

4 TBSP BUTTER (UNSALTED)

3 TBSP MAPLE SYRUP

3 TBSP HEAVY WHIPPING CREAM

½ CUP POWDERED SUGAR

3 TBSP PECANS, FINE CHOP

Apple Crisp

 Apple crisp will always remind me of the cozy evenings spent at my Aunt Trish's house. My cousins and I were in our twenties, and we got together at her house on Sundays. We'd gather in her kitchen, peel apples, mix up the topping, and bake it all together—her apple crisp recipe quickly became a favorite. One night still makes us laugh. My aunt's husband had gone on a goose hunt and got one. He was so proud and wanted to make a goose dinner for us. While we all tried our best to eat it, let's just say it wasn't the highlight of the meal. Thankfully, the apple crisp was there to save the night—warm, comforting, and so delicious. It's still one of those recipes that brings everyone to the table and keeps the memories (and laughter) going.

INGREDIENTS

4 CUPS APPLES, PEELED AND SLICED (CORTLAND OR MACINTOSH)

¼ CUP ORANGE JUICE

1 CUP SUGAR

¾ CUP FLOUR

½ TSP CINNAMON

¼ TSP NUTMEG

DASH OF SALT

½ CUP UNSALTED BUTTER, ROOM TEMPERATURE

PREPARATION

1. Preheat oven to 375°F.
2. Place the apples in a baking dish and pour the orange juice over them.
3. Mix all dry ingredients together in a bowl.
4. Cut room-temperature butter into the dry ingredients with a fork or a pastry blender until it reaches the consistency of coarse meal.
5. Sprinkle the mixture evenly over the apples.
6. Bake at 375°F for 45 to 50 minutes.
7. Enjoy with ice cream.

Pistachio Cake & Icing

INGREDIENTS

- **1** BOX YELLOW CAKE MIX
- **1** PACKAGE OF INSTANT PISTACHIO (PUDDING MIX)
- **4** EGGS
- **¾** CUP VEGETABLE OIL
- **¾** CUP WATER
- **1-½** TSP ALMOND EXTRACT

CAKE PREPARATION

1. Preheat oven to 350°F. Spray a 10-inch Bundt pan with baking spray.
2. Mix all ingredients until well blended.
3. Pour cake batter into the Bundt pan and bake for 40-45 minutes (toothpick will come out clean when done).

Enjoy!

INGREDIENTS

- **1** CUP CONFECTIONERS' SUGAR
- **2** TBSP WATER
- SPLASH OF ALMOND EXTRACT

ICING PREPARATION

1. Mix confectioners' sugar, water, and almond extract together.
2. Wait for the cake to cool completely then drizzle icing over the cake.

Enjoy!

Pistachio cake with icing is a recipe I got from my very good friend, Jess Patten. While Jess makes it a little differently by adding a layer of cinnamon, sugar, and walnuts, it's still just as delicious, and I love making it for people. The subtle, nutty flavor of the pistachios combined with the sweet icing makes it a unique and comforting treat. It's one of those cakes that's always a crowd-pleaser, and I enjoy sharing it with friends and family.

ALWAYS ALLIE

Pumpkin Pie

INGREDIENTS

1 PIE CRUST

12-OUNCE CAN EVAPORATED MILK

¾ CUP SUGAR

¼ TSP SALT

1 TSP GROUND CINNAMON

1 TSP GROUND GINGER

½ TSP GROUND NUTMEG

¼ TSP GROUND CLOVES

2 LARGE EGGS

1 CAN PURE PUMPKIN PUREE

PREPARATION

1. Preheat oven to 425°F.
2. Blind-bake your pie crust for 15 minutes.
3. Pour evaporated milk into a mixing bowl. Add all dry ingredients and mix well.
4. Beat the eggs in a separate bowl, then add them to the milk and spice mixture. Add the pumpkin and mix well with a whisk.
5. Pour pie mixture into the prepared pie crust.
6. Bake at 425°F for 15 minutes. Reduce the temperature to 350°F and bake for 40 minutes. Cool for 2 hours. Serve with whipped cream.

   Enjoy!

Mulled Apple Cider

INGREDIENTS

½ GALLON APPLE CIDER

1 CUP ORANGE JUICE

2 STICKS OF CINNAMON

¼ TSP GROUND CLOVES

¼ TSP GROUND ALLSPICE

3 PODS OF STAR ANISE

6 SLICES OF FRESH ORANGES

RUM OR BOURBON, IF DESIRED

PREPARATION

1. Place all ingredients in a large stockpot and bring to a simmer. Cover, reduce heat, and let marry for 15 to 30 minutes.

2. If you wish, you can strain the cider, but this is not necessary. Ladle into your desired mug, and garnish with cinnamon sticks, orange slices, and star anise pods. Add rum or bourbon, if desired.

3. The cider can be left on the stovetop over very low heat to keep warm, or you can transfer it to a slow cooker and keep it on low. Feel free to add rum or bourbon, if desired.

Enjoy!

Espresso Martini

INGREDIENTS

1 OUNCE COFFEE LIQUOR (KAHLUA)

2 OUNCES VODKA

1 OUNCE FRESHLY BREWED ESPRESSO (STILL WARM IS FINE)

3 WHOLE COFFEE BEANS FOR GARNISH

PREPARATION

1. Add coffee liquor, measured-out vodka, espresso, and simple syrup to a shaker filled with crushed ice.

2. Shake vigorously for a minute, then strain into a chilled martini glass.

3. Garnish with 3 coffee beans and serve.

   Enjoy!

Espresso martinis have become one of our favorite drinks, thanks to a local restaurant in Portsmouth, New Hampshire, where we discovered how perfect they can be. We got to know Rob, the bartender there, who crafted them with such skill that they were nothing short of magic. After becoming good friends with him, he was kind enough to share his recipe, and now I make them at home for us and our friends. They've become a huge hit at every gathering, with everyone always asking for more. It's one of those drinks that's not only delicious but also adds a special touch to any evening.

RECIPE BOOK

The View in Tuscany!

ALWAYS ALLIE

About the Author

Photo by Izzy

Allie Always is always busy - whether in the kitchen, around the home, or traveling the world. It's no coincidence that one friend gave her the nickname Allie Always. She shares her recipes, travel tips, and general lifestyle advice with fellow busy readers on the Allie Always blog.

Family is a key part of Allie's life. As a young girl, she developed a love of cooking while spending time with both of her grandmothers. She continues sharing her love of cooking with friends and family. With an emphasis on family-style meals, Allie Always' cooking style brings flavor and excitement to healthy meals. Allie and her husband, Corey, raised their daughter to be a foodie just like them.

Outside of her kitchen, Allie Always enjoys gardening, with the fruits of her labor ending up in her favorite recipes. Allie shares her love of cooking with others by teaching a cooking class and a summer camp at her daughter's school. She works with Corey in their shared business.

When not cooking at home, Allie enjoys traveling and trying new foods, the best of which she brings back to her home kitchen to recreate. She shows other busy home cooks that cooking can be both fun and easy.

Allie and Family at Wentworth Coolidge Mansion

Index

A

8	Allie's Avocado Toast
116	Allie's Buddha Bowl
3	Allie's Detox Green Juice
21	Apple Cider Vinegar Dressing
203	Apple Crisp
25	Avocado Dressing

B

91	Baby Spinach and Berry Salad
72	Baked Macaroni and Smoked Cheese
22	Balsamic Dressing
34	Beef Bone Broth
177	Beef Stew
131	Beef, Cabbage, and Barley Soup
15	Blueberry Muffins
96	Blueberry, Kale, & Candied Pecan Salad
109	Bowls (Section 5)
174	Braised Beef Short Ribs
189	Breads (Section 7)
45	Burrata Cheese Peaches on Sourdough Bread
191	But You Ain't Ever Had My Cornbread
158	Butternut Squash and Spinach Lasagna Rolls
123	Butternut Squash Soup with
124	Cranberry and Apple Relish

C

166	Cajun Shrimp Foils
111	Cali Shrimp Bowls
178	Canadian Meat Pie (Tourtière)
11	Chia Seed Pudding Bowls
148	Chicken and White Bean Chili
182	Chicken Cacciatore
136	Chicken Noodle Soup
165	Chicken Pot Pie
173	Chicken Tacos
109	Chilis (Section 5)
196	Chocolate Chip Banana Bread
161	Coconut Curry Shrimp with Cilantro Lime Rice
128	Coconut, Curry, Lime, & Chicken Soup

RECIPE BOOK

Index

30	Corey and Allie's BBQ Rub
57	Cottage Cheese Party Dip
112	Crispy Chickpea Bowl

D
189	Desserts (Section 7)
19	Dressings (Section 2)
189	Drinks (Section 7)

E
170	Easy Mushroom Risotto
211	Espresso Martini

F
95	Fall Harvest Salad
192	Focaccia Bread
37	Fresh Basil Pesto
66	Fresh Mex Tomatillo Salsa

G
84	Greek Pasta Salad
162	Ground Turkey & Sweet Potato Skillet
54	Guacamole

H
154	Ham and Broccoli Quiche
115	Harvest Bowl
4	Healthy Banana, Oatmeal, Dark Chocolate Chip Bites
80	Healthy Broccoli Slaw

I
83	Italian Pasta Salad

J
181	Jambalaya

M
151	Mains (Section 6)
99	Mandarin Orange Salad
65	Mango Salsa
87	Mediterranean Orzo Salad
71	Mexican Street Corn
26	Miso Dressing
208	Mulled Apple Cider

N
29	North Carolina BBQ Sauce

Index

P

169	Pan Seared Scallops
49	Party Ranch Oyster Crackers
16	Pecan Cinnamon Twists
19	Pickled (Section 2)
38	Pickled Jalapenos
41	Pickled Red Onions
204	Pistachio Cake With Icing
62	Pizza Pinwheels
120	Potato and Leek Soup
88	Potato Salad
200	Pumpkin Bundt Cake with Maple Pecan Glaze
207	Pumpkin Pie
143	Pumpkin, Kale, and Quinoa Soup

R

199	Red Velvet Cupcakes with Cream Cheese Frosting
104	Roasted Beet and Baby Kale Salad
144	Roasted Eggplant & Red Pepper Soup
119	Roasted Sweet Potato Bowl with Farro
135	Roasted Tomato Soup
19	Rubs (Section 2)

S

69	Salads (Section 4)
19	Sauces (Section 2)
127	Sausage Tortellini Soup
76	Sautéed Snow Peas
53	Seven-Layer Taco Dip
92	Shrimp, Mango, and Avocado Salad
185	Shrimp, Sausage, and Rice Skillet
69	Sides (Section 4)
109	Soups (Section 5)
79	Southern Coleslaw
75	Southern Green Beans & Salt Pork
12	Southern Sausage Gravy
50	Spicy Maple Candied Bacon
139	Split Pea and Ham Soup
1	Start of Day (Section 1)
45	Starters (Section 3)
107	Strawberry, Spinach, & Chicken Salad

157	Stuffed Butternut Squash
153	Stuffed Peppers
186	Sweet Potato & Black Bean Burger
147	Sweet Potato and Ground Turkey Chili

T

103	Taco Salad
33	Taco Seasoning
7	The Best Protein Bars
46	Tomato Confit With Whipped Ricotta Cheese
61	Tortellini Caprese Skewers
140	Turkey, Mushroom, and Barley Soup

W

100	Watermelon and Tomato Salad
58	Whipped Ricotta & Heirloom Tomatoes
132	White Bean and Kale Soup

Z

195	Zucchini Chocolate Chip Bread

www.ingramcontent.com/pod-product-compliance
Lightning Source LLC
Chambersburg PA
CBHW041150060526
44107CB00141B/1108